הגדה של פסח
Haggadah for Pesach

Annotated Edition

With an English Translation by
Rabbi Jacob Immanuel Schochet

Published by
MERKOS L'INYONEI CHINUCH
770 Eastern Parkway, Brooklyn, New York 11213
5770 · 2010

HAGGADAH FOR PESACH
ANNOTATED EDITION
Copyright © 2005
Second Printing—March 2007
Third Printing—February 2008
Fourth Printing—January 2010
by
MERKOS L'INYONEI CHINUCH, INC.
770 Eastern Parkway / Brooklyn, New York 11213
(718) 774-4000 / FAX (718) 774-2718
editor@kehot.com

ORDER DEPARTMENT
291 Kingston Avenue / Brooklyn, New York 11213
(718) 778-0226 / FAX (718) 778-4148
www.kehot.com

ISBN: 978-0-8266-0162-9

Printed in Canada

Contents

Preface

*W*ith thanks to the Almighty, we proudly present the *Haggadah for Pesach—Annotated Edition*, arranged according to the text of Rabbi Schneur Zalman of Liadi.

In this Haggadah, each part of the Pesach Seder is illuminated with clear, step-by-step instructions. These detailed instructions, culled from the Haggadah commentary authored by the Lubavitcher Rebbe, Rabbi Menachem M. Schneerson, of righteous memory, guide the Seder participant through the often-times complicated order of the Seder. Rabbi Schneur Zalman's original Hebrew instructions also appear in the Hebrew text.[1]

To further enhance the user-friendliness of this Haggadah, we have completely reset the Hebrew and English texts in crisp, clear type. Selected transliterations appear at the end of this volume.

The reader is encouraged to take note of the section called *Terms and Measurements for the Seder*. This section contains important information, and should be read prior to preparing for the Seder.

It is hoped that this new edition of the *Haggadah for Pesach* will enhance our celebration of the Festival of our Redemption, which serves as a prelude to the ultimate redemption by Moshiach, may it be speedily in our days.

Merkos L'Inyonei Chinuch

Rosh Chodesh Nissan 5765

---

1. Note that these may sometimes differ from the English instructions, as the latter are based on actual Chabad practice. For a discussion of these differences, see *Haggadah for Pesach with an Anthology of Reasons and Customs* (Kehot, 2004).

Introduction

Pesach: Its Timeless Message

*T*here is hardly another date in our calendar so rich in tradition, customs, historical involvement and symbolism, as the Festival of Pesach. For Pesach marks our exodus from Egypt, the birth of our nation.[1]

We are enjoined to "remember the day of your leaving Egypt, all the days of your life."[2] In every generation, indeed every day, each one must regard himself as if he himself had that day come out of Egypt.[3] This experience of liberation and freedom really comes alive on Pesach, especially at the Seder.

When conducting the Seder we relive the story of the exodus by recalling that event in all its details, and by eating matzah and maror even as our ancestors did "in those days, at this time." We forge the links with our past and our future, as we fulfill the precept of "You shall tell your child on that day, saying: It is because of this, that God did for me when I went out from Egypt."[4]

At the Seder, when reciting the Haggadah, Pesach generates *"pe sach*—the mouth relates" the story of the exodus;[5] the matzah is transformed from *"lechem oni*—the bread of afflic-

---

1. Ezekiel 16:4. See the commentaries there.
2. Deuteronomy 16:3. See *Berachot* 12b (cited in the Haggadah, pp. 42-43). See also Rashi on Exodus 13:3; *Rambam, Hilchot Keriat Shema* 1:3; *Shulchan Aruch Harav, Orach Chayim* 67:1.
3. *Pesachim* 116b (cited in the Haggadah, pp. 62-63); *Tanya,* ch. 47.
4. Exodus 13:8 (cited in the Haggadah, pp. 44-45).
5. R. Chaim Vital, *Peri Eitz Chayim, Sha'ar Chag Hamatzot,* ch. 7; *Sha'ar Hakavanot, Inyan Hapesach, derush* 3. See also *Chida, Devash Lefi, s.v. Peh,* par. 6.

tion" to "*lechem oni*—the bread of response," that is, the bread causing many things to be asked, answered and discussed.[6]

Our Sages composed for us the Haggadah, a text offering all the significant details of the historical miracle of the exodus that are to be remembered, retold and relived on this glorious night of the Seder—"so that you will tell in the ears of your child and your grandchild that which I wrought in Egypt, and My signs which I have done among them; and you will know that I am God!"[7]

For the Seder to be an authentic experience, then, it is not enough to simply recite the Haggadah. One must understand it and probe its contents. One must sense and live the proceedings. "Everyone must bestir himself with awe to follow the instructions of the Sages who arranged the precept of the Seder and the Haggadah. This matter should not be trivial in one's eyes! There are some things at the Seder which may seem insignificant to man, but let him act prudently to observe them—for there is nothing vain among them!"[8]

In this context, I translated the whole Haggadah according to the authoritative text found in the Siddur of the Alter Rebbe, R. Schneur Zalman of Liadi.

Comments on Translation

a. As the Haggadah is a liturgical text, I chose to render the *Shem Havayah* (Tetragrammaton) as GOD (in capital letters).

b. Various precepts observed at the Seder are subject to specific Halachic measurements. For the convenience of those using this Haggadah, the *Terms and Measurements* following the *Introduction* offer a practical guide to these measurements, as well as some helpful suggestions.[9]

---

6. *Pesachim* 36a and 115b, interpreting Deuteronomy 16:3.
7. Exodus 10:2.
8. *Sefer Maharil,* beginning of *Hilchot Hahaggadah.*
9. These measurements are based on *Shulchan Aruch, Orach Chayim* sect. 486 (with equivalent amounts etc. taken from Rabbi A. C. Noeh, *Kuntres*

c. Some Hebrew words and terms are generally left untranslated. The *Glossary* appended offers their translations and some explanations.

⁓

The proper observance of Pesach is a most beautiful and inspiring experience, though not always too easy. There are very strict requirements to remove all traces of chametz from our possession, and to prevent any contact with it. We need special zeal to preserve the ritual purity of Pesach throughout its duration.

On the other hand, "commensurate with the painstaking effort is the reward."[10] The special care and zeal to be manifest on Pesach reflects itself throughout the year. Thus said R. Yitzchak Luria, that he who is very meticulous in these requirements is assured safeguarding against any unwitting sin throughout the year.[11]

As we recall and relive our redemption from the *Mitzrayim* (Egypt) of old, may we all merit very soon to be redeemed from the *meytzarim*—the straits and constrictions—of the present, speedily to experience the literal fulfillment of, "As in the days of your going out from Egypt, I will show them wondrous things!"[12]

J. Immanuel Schochet

Hashiurim, s.v. revi'it, kezayit, and *achilat peras);* Responsa of *Tzemach Tzedek* (Kehot, 1994), *Orach Chayim,* no. 108 (text and gloss). The late Rabbi Zalman S. Dworkin, Rav of the Lubavitch community, reviewed and ratified these measurements.

10. *Avot* 5:21. See *Zohar* III: 278b.

11. *Devash Lefi, s.v. Chet,* par. 18; *Ba'er Heitev, Orach Chayim* 447: note 1. See *Zohar* III:282b; *Likkutei Sichot* III: p. 945.

12. Micah 7:15.

Terms and Measurements for the Seder

S pecific instructions for the proceedings of the Seder are offered in the appropriate places of the Haggadah. It is important, though, to be aware of the proper measures for the various requirements.

Four Cups of Wine

Four cups of wine are to be drunk during the Seder, by both men and women. The minimum size for each cup is a *revi'it* (lit., one fourth [of a *log*]), which is about 3.5 fluid ounces (nearly 105 milliliters).[1] Ideally one should drink the *whole cup* each time; if this is not possible, one is to drink at least a little more than half of the cup. It is better to use a smaller cup (with minimum size) and to drink the whole cup, than using a larger one and not drinking all of it.

Karpas

One should eat *less* than a *kezayit* (a fraction less than an ounce, nearly 26 gram) of the Karpas, that is, not more than half an ounce.

Matzah

Matzah must be eaten three times during the Seder:

1. The first time at the beginning of the meal, after reciting the Motzi and the special blessing for the matzah. This initial consumption of matzah is a Biblical precept *(de'orayta),* and thus more stringent. For this initial consumption one

---

1. Actually the precise amount (according to Rabbi Noeh's calculation) is 86 milliliters (2.9 fluid oz), which one may rely on. In view of more common practice I rounded it off upward to the size mentioned.

is to use two *kezeitim:* one *kezayit* of the top matzah, and one *kezayit* of the middle (broken) matzah. However, by Biblical precept only one *kezayit* need be consumed, while the other *kezayit is* a Rabbinic precept *(derabanan).* Practically speaking this means:

One *kezayit* matzah is a fraction less than one ounce (25.6 gram). It is to be remembered, though, that in chewing the matzah, some particles will crumble, and some remain between the teeth, and are not swallowed; thus one should take a little bit more than the size stated to assure the swallowing of a whole *kezayit.*

In terms of spatial dimensions:

Machine-baked matzot are generally of uniform size and weight (approximately 1.2 ounces, or 36 gram). Hand-baked matzot vary in both size and density. Nonetheless, the *average* hand-baked matzah has a diameter of 10-10 1/2 inches, and weighs 2.3 ounces (66 gram). One *kezayit* matzah (slightly less than one ounce) is then a piece of 5 by 7 inches in area.

If someone should find it difficult to consume two *kezeitim* of this size, one may use a smaller amount for the second *kezayit* (which, as stated, is *derabanan),* namely about two-thirds of an ounce (17.3 gram), thus a third less than the first *kezayit* (or roughly 4 by 6 inches*).*

2. The second time, is the matzah used for Korech—the sandwich of matzah and maror. This, too, is a Rabbinic precept *(derabanan).* Thus here, too, if *it is difficult* to follow the stricter measure of approximately one ounce, one may suffice with just two-thirds of an ounce (17.3 gram) of matzah.

3. The third time one is to eat matzah is the afikoman, of which one should ideally consume two *kezeitim.* If this is difficult, one *kezayit* is enough. Eating the afikoman is also *derabanan,* thus if unable to consume the full size for a *kezayit,* one may suffice with the smaller size of two-thirds of an ounce (17.3 gram) per *kezayit.*

Note: In each of these three cases one should complete

the consumption of the required amount in *four to seven minutes.*

Maror

Since the destruction of the *Beit Hamikdash* and the consequent absence of the Pesach offering, the precept of eating bitter herbs is *derabanan.* Thus one may suffice with the smaller measure of a *kezayit,* namely two-thirds of an ounce (17.3 gram).

This applies to the original consumption of maror by itself, as well as for the maror used for Korech.

For both Maror and Korech it is our custom to use a mixture of horseradish and chazeret (lettuce) to make up the required amount of a *kezayit.* When using the stems of romaine lettuce, however, the amount for a *kezayit is* slightly higher—namely a little *more* than 2/3 of an ounce (19.2 gram).

Note: For both Maror and Korech one should complete the consumption of the required amount in *four to seven minutes.*

Suggestions for the Seder

Matzah

Only three matzot are placed on the Seder plate, and generally not everyone has his/her own Seder plate. This means that the leader of the Seder has to distribute the required amounts for all participants from his matzot. The three matzot, thus, will obviously not be sufficient for everyone; and certainly not for the afikoman, which is itself just more than half a matzah. However, when it comes to distributing matzah for Motzi, Korech and afikoman, one can supplement the original matzot with others which should be prepared beforehand.

It is advisable to prepare with care pieces of matzah in the

proper sizes before the Seder, and to keep them near the leader, so that they can then be distributed with smaller pieces from the Seder plate at the appropriate times.

Zeroa

It is customary to take a section of a fowl's neck bone. We are particular not to eat of the zeroa, so as to avoid any similarity to the Pesach-offering. It is therefore preferable to remove almost all the flesh from the zeroa.

Chazeret

The prevalent custom is to use romaine lettuce for chazeret. Some use endives or iceberg lettuce. When using such leaves, especially romaine lettuce, one must be *careful to check them for insects* before the Seder. Many insects are very small, the same color as the leaves, and thus difficult to detect. It is advisable, therefore, to use only the center ribs, as they can be examined and cleaned much more easily, rather than whole leaves.

Additional Note

On the eve of Pesach one is not allowed to eat any matzah (and also on the first day of Pesach one should limit the eating of matzah), so that when eating matzah at the Seder (to fulfill the mitzvah) it will be a conspicuous event and one will do so with proper appetite. For the same reason one should not eat maror on the eve of Pesach and on the first day. Moreover, it is our custom not to eat matzah during the 30 days preceding Pesach.

It is also our custom that from the morning of the eve of Pesach, until after the Korech of the second Seder, one does not eat any of the ingredients of the charoset and maror.

Preparing
for
Pesach

סדר בדיקת חמץ

There is a Biblical prohibition against owning or even possessing chametz (leavened products) on Pesach. To help facilitate the removal of one's chametz, the Sages instituted the "Search For Chametz" on the eve of the Fourteenth of Nissan (the night before the Seder), and the burning of chametz on the following morning. During this search, one carefully inspects the entire home (and all other properties, e.g., one's car, office, etc.) for any chametz that might be scattered about.

When Erev Pesach coincides with Shabbat, the search and burning of chametz are moved up to Thursday evening and Friday morning respectively.

It is customary to put pieces of bread—wrapped in paper to prevent crumbling—in various places around the house, so that the one who searches will find them. According to Kabbalah, ten pieces should be used.

The search is performed by the light of a wax candle (customarily beeswax), and with a bird's feather. The chametz found during the search is put into a paper bag.

One is to search in all hidden places, even cracks in the floor.

One is not to speak between the blessing and the beginning of the search, even concerning the search itself. Once the search begins, one may only speak about things that are relevant to the search.

The search is performed by the head of the household, who recites the blessing. Members of the household participating in the search should stand nearby to hear the blessing, and should immediately begin their search by inspecting an area in the room nearest the place where the blessing was heard. They should then proceed to search their own designated area—all without speaking in between.

Before the search, the following blessing is recited while holding the lit candle:

בָּרוּךְ אַתָּה יְיָ אֱלֹהֵינוּ מֶלֶךְ הָעוֹלָם, אֲשֶׁר קִדְּשָׁנוּ
בְּמִצְוֹתָיו, וְצִוָּנוּ עַל בִּעוּר חָמֵץ: (אָמֵן —Listeners)

After the search, the remainder of the candle and the feather are placed in the bag, which is placed in the bowl of a wooden spoon. These are then wrapped in paper, tied with a string, and knotted around the handle of the spoon, which remains uncovered. One must be careful that the chametz retained (to be eaten or to be burnt in the morning) should be put in a safe place, so that it is not carried about and thereby crumbled and spread by children or rodents.

After the search one must also nullify the chametz he may have overlooked and say:

כָּל חֲמִירָא וַחֲמִיעָא דְּאִכָּא בִרְשׁוּתִי, דְּלָא חֲמִיתֵיה
וּדְלָא בְעַרְתֵּיה וּדְלָא יְדַעְנָא לֵיה, לִבָּטֵל וְלֶהֱוֵי
הֶפְקֵר כְּעַפְרָא דְאַרְעָא:

The nullification must be done with full awareness of the act. Therefore, one who does not understand the Aramaic text must recite it in a language he does understand.

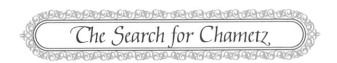

The Search for Chametz

There is a Biblical prohibition against owning or even possessing chametz (leavened products) on Pesach. To help facilitate the removal of one's chametz, the Sages instituted the "Search For Chametz" on the eve of the Fourteenth of Nissan (the night before the Seder), and the burning of chametz on the following morning. During this search, one carefully inspects the entire home (and all other properties, e.g., one's car, office, etc.) for any chametz that might be scattered about.

When Erev Pesach coincides with Shabbat, the search and burning of chametz are moved up to Thursday evening and Friday morning respectively.

It is customary to put pieces of bread—wrapped in paper to prevent crumbling—in various places around the house, so that the one who searches will find them. According to Kabbalah, ten pieces should be used.

The search is performed by the light of a wax candle (customarily beeswax), and with a bird's feather. The chametz found during the search is put into a paper bag.

One is to search in all hidden places, even cracks in the floor.

One is not to speak between the blessing and the beginning of the search, even concerning the search itself. Once the search begins, one may only speak about things that are relevant to the search.

The search is performed by the head of the household, who recites the blessing. Members of the household participating in the search should stand nearby to hear the blessing, and should immediatly begin their search by inspecting an area in the room nearest the place where the blessing was heard. They should then proceed to search their own designated area—all without speaking in between.

Before the search, the following blessing is recited while holding the lit candle:

ברוך Blessed are You, GOD, our God, King of the universe, who has sanctified us with His commandments and commanded us concerning the removal of chametz.

(Listeners—Amen.)

After the search, the remainder of the candle and the feather are placed in the bag, which is placed in the bowl of a wooden spoon. These are then wrapped in paper, tied with a string, and knotted around the handle of the spoon, which remains uncovered. One must be careful that the chametz retained (to be eaten or to be burnt in the morning) should be put in a safe place, so that it is not carried about and thereby crumbled and spread by children or rodents.

After the search one must also nullify the chametz he may have overlooked and say:

כל All leaven and anything leavened that is in my possession, which I have neither seen nor removed, and about which I am unaware, shall be considered nullified and ownerless as the dust of the earth.

The nullification must be done with full awareness of the act. Therefore, one who does not understand the Aramaic text must recite it in a language he does understand.

סדר ביעור חמץ

The chametz, including the ten pieces, should be burned in a fire on the morning of the fourteenth of Nissan. Consult a Jewish calendar for the specific time to burn the chametz in your area.

After placing the chametz in the fire, one should recite the following declaration, nullifying any remaining chametz:

כָּל חֲמִירָא וַחֲמִיעָא דְּאִכָּא בִרְשׁוּתִי, דַּחֲזִיתֵיהּ וּדְלָא חֲזִיתֵיהּ, דַּחֲמִיתֵיהּ וּדְלָא חֲמִיתֵיהּ, דְּבִעַרְתֵּיהּ וּדְלָא בִעַרְתֵּיהּ, לִבָּטֵל וְלֶהֱוֵי הֶפְקֵר כְּעַפְרָא דְאַרְעָא:

The following is said during the burning of the chametz:

יְהִי רָצוֹן מִלְּפָנֶיךָ יְיָ אֱלֹהֵינוּ וֵאלֹהֵי אֲבוֹתֵינוּ, כְּשֵׁם שֶׁאֲנִי מְבַעֵר חָמֵץ מִבֵּיתִי וּמֵרְשׁוּתִי, כַּךְ תְּבַעֵר אֶת כָּל הַחִיצוֹנִים, וְאֶת רוּחַ הַטֻּמְאָה תַּעֲבִיר מִן הָאָרֶץ, וְאֶת יִצְרֵנוּ הָרָע תַּעֲבִירֵהוּ מֵאִתָּנוּ, וְתִתֶּן לָנוּ לֵב בָּשָׂר לְעָבְדְּךָ בֶּאֱמֶת, וְכָל סִטְרָא אָחֳרָא וְכָל הַקְּלִפּוֹת וְכָל הָרִשְׁעָה בְּעָשָׁן תִּכְלֶה, וְתַעֲבִיר מֶמְשֶׁלֶת זָדוֹן מִן הָאָרֶץ, וְכָל הַמְּעִיקִים לַשְּׁכִינָה תְּבַעֲרֵם בְּרוּחַ בָּעֵר וּבְרוּחַ מִשְׁפָּט כְּשֵׁם שֶׁבִּעַרְתָּ אֶת מִצְרַיִם וְאֶת אֱלֹהֵיהֶם בַּיָּמִים הָהֵם בִּזְמַן הַזֶּה, אָמֵן סֶלָה:

סדר קרבן פסח

"We offer the words of our lips in place of the sacrifice of bullocks." The Minchah prayer takes the place of the daily afternoon offering; and in the time of the *Beit Hamikdash*, the Pesach offering was sacrificed after the daily afternoon offering. Thus

Burning the Chametz

The chametz, including the ten pieces, should be burned in a fire on the morning of the fourteenth of Nissan. Consult a Jewish calendar for the specific time to burn the chametz in your area.

After placing the chametz in the fire, one should recite the following declaration, nullifying any remaining chametz:

כל All leaven and anything leavened that is in my possession, whether I have seen it or not, whether I have observed it or not, whether I have removed it or not, shall be considered nullified and ownerless as the dust of the earth.

The following is said during the burning of the chametz:

יהי May it be Your will, GOD, our God and God of our fathers, that just as I remove the chametz from my house and from my possession, so shall You remove all the extraneous forces. Remove the spirit of impurity from the earth, remove our evil inclination from us, and grant us a heart of flesh to serve You in truth. Make all the *sitra achara,* all the *kelipot,* and all wickedness be consumed in smoke, and remove the dominion of evil from the earth. Remove with a spirit of destruction and a spirit of judgment all that distress the Shechinah, just as You destroyed Egypt and its idols in those days, at this time. Amen, *Selah.*

Order of the Pesach Offering

"We offer the words of our lips in place of the sacrifice of bullocks." The Minchah prayer takes the place of the daily afternoon offering; and in the time of the *Beit Hamikdash,* the Pesach offering was sacrificed after the daily afternoon offering. Thus

it is appropriate to study the order of the Pesach offering after Minchah, by saying the following:

קָרְבַּן פֶּסַח מֵבִיא מִן הַכְּבָשִׂים אוֹ מִן הָעִזִּים זָכָר בֶּן שָׁנָה, וְשׁוֹחֲטוֹ בָּעֲזָרָה בְּכָל מָקוֹם, אַחַר חֲצוֹת אַרְבָּעָה עָשָׂר דַּוְקָא, וְאַחַר שְׁחִיטַת תָּמִיד שֶׁל בֵּין הָעַרְבַּיִם, וְאַחַר הֲטָבַת נֵרוֹת שֶׁל בֵּין הָעַרְבַּיִם. וְאֵין שׁוֹחֲטִין אֶת הַפֶּסַח עַל הֶחָמֵץ. וְאִם שָׁחַט קוֹדֶם לַתָּמִיד, כָּשֵׁר, וּבִלְבַד שֶׁיְּהֵא אַחֵר מְמָרֵס בְּדַם הַפֶּסַח כְּדֵי שֶׁלֹּא יִקְרַשׁ עַד שֶׁיִּזְרְקוּ דַם הַתָּמִיד, וְאַחַר כָּךְ יִזְרְקוּ דַם הַפֶּסַח זְרִיקָה אַחַת כְּנֶגֶד הַיְסוֹד. וְכֵיצַד עוֹשִׂין? שָׁחַט הַשּׁוֹחֵט, וְקִבֵּל הַכֹּהֵן הָרִאשׁוֹן שֶׁבָּרֹאשׁ הַשּׁוּרָה וְנָתַן לַחֲבֵרוֹ, וַחֲבֵרוֹ לַחֲבֵרוֹ, וְהַכֹּהֵן הַקָּרוֹב אֵצֶל הַמִּזְבֵּחַ זוֹרְקוֹ זְרִיקָה אַחַת כְּנֶגֶד הַיְסוֹד, וְחוֹזֵר הַכְּלִי רֵיקָן לַחֲבֵרוֹ, וַחֲבֵרוֹ לַחֲבֵרוֹ, וּמְקַבֵּל כְּלִי הַמָּלֵא תְחִלָּה וְאַחַר כָּךְ מַחֲזִיר הָרֵיקָן. וְהָיוּ שׁוּרוֹת שֶׁל בָּזִיכֵי כֶסֶף וְשׁוּרוֹת שֶׁל בָּזִיכֵי זָהָב. וְלֹא הָיוּ לַבָּזִיכִין שׁוּלַיִם, שֶׁמָּא יַנִּיחֵם וְיִקְרַשׁ הַדָּם. אַחַר כָּךְ תּוֹלִין אֶת הַפֶּסַח וּמַפְשִׁיטִין אוֹתוֹ כֻּלּוֹ, וְקוֹרְעִין אוֹתוֹ, וּמְמַחִין אֶת קְרָבָיו עַד שֶׁיֵּצֵא הַפֶּרֶשׁ, וּמוֹצִיאִין אֶת הָאֵמוּרִים, וְהֵם: הַחֵלֶב שֶׁעַל הַקֶּרֶב, וְיוֹתֶרֶת הַכָּבֵד, וּשְׁתֵּי כְלָיוֹת וְהַחֵלֶב שֶׁעֲלֵיהֶן, וְהָאַלְיָה לְעֻמַּת הֶעָצֶה, וְנוֹתְנָם בִּכְלִי שָׁרֵת, וּמוֹלְחָם וּמַקְטִירָם הַכֹּהֵן עַל גַּבֵּי הַמִּזְבֵּחַ כָּל אֶחָד לְבַדּוֹ. וְהַשְּׁחִיטָה וְהַזְּרִיקָה וּמִחוּי קְרָבָיו וְהֶקְטֵר חֲלָבָיו דּוֹחִין אֶת הַשַּׁבָּת, וּשְׁאָר עִנְיָנָיו אֵינָם דּוֹחִין אֶת הַשַּׁבָּת. וְכֵן אֵין מוֹלִיכִין אֶת הַפֶּסַח לַבַּיִת כְּשֶׁחָל בְּשַׁבָּת, אֶלָּא כַּת הָאַחַת הֵם מִתְעַכְּבִים עִם פִּסְחֵיהֶם

it is appropriate to study the order of the Pesach offering after Minchah, by saying the following:

קָרְבָּן The Pesach offering is brought from yearling male lambs or goats, and slaughtered anywhere in the Temple court only after midday of the fourteenth of Nissan, after the slaughtering of the daily afternoon offering and after the afternoon cleaning of the cups of the menorah. One should not slaughter the Pesach offering while chametz is in his possession. If he slaughtered it before the daily afternoon offering, it is acceptable, provided that someone stir the blood of the Pesach offering so that it will not congeal until the blood of the daily afternoon offering will have been sprinkled, and then the blood of the Pesach offering is sprinkled once toward the base of the altar. How is it done? The *shochet* slaughters it, and the first Kohen at the head of the line receives it and hands it over to his colleague, and his colleague to his colleague, and the Kohen nearest the altar sprinkles it once toward the base of the altar. He returns the empty vessel to his colleague, and his colleague to his colleague, receiving first the full vessel and then returning the empty one. There were rows of silver vessels and rows of golden vessels, and the vessels did not have flat bottoms lest they set them down and the blood become congealed. Afterwards they hung the Pesach offering, flayed it completely, tore it open, and cleansed its bowels until the wastes were removed. They took out the parts offered on the altar, namely, the fat that is on the entrails, the lobe of the liver, the two kidneys with the fat on them, and the tail up to the backbone, and placed them in a ritual vessel. The Kohen then salted them and burned them upon the altar, each one individually. The slaughtering, the sprinkling of its blood, the cleansing of its bowels and the burning of its fat override the Shabbat, but other things pertaining to it do not override the Shabbat. Likewise, if [the fourteenth of Nissan] occurs on Shabbat, the Pesach offerings are not carried home, but one group remains with their Pesach offerings on

בְּהַר הַבַּיִת, וְהַכַּת הַשְּׁנִיָּה יוֹשֶׁבֶת לָהּ בַּחֵיל, וְהַשְּׁלִישִׁית בִּמְקוֹמָהּ עוֹמֶדֶת. חָשְׁכָה, יָצְאוּ וְצָלוּ פִּסְחֵיהֶם. בִּשְׁלֹשָׁה כִתּוֹת הַפֶּסַח נִשְׁחָט, וְאֵין כַּת פְּחוּתָה מִשְּׁלֹשִׁים אֲנָשִׁים. נִכְנְסָה כַּת הָרִאשׁוֹנָה, נִתְמַלְּאָה הָעֲזָרָה, נוֹעֲלִין אוֹתָהּ. וּבְעוֹד שֶׁהֵם שׁוֹחֲטִין וּמַקְרִיבִין אֶת הָאֵימוּרִים, קוֹרְאִין אֶת הַהַלֵּל. אִם גָּמְרוּ אוֹתוֹ קוֹדֶם שֶׁיַּקְרִיבוּ כֻּלָּם, שׁוֹנִים אוֹתוֹ, וְאִם שָׁנוּ יְשַׁלֵּשׁוּ. עַל כָּל קְרִיאָה תּוֹקְעִין שָׁלֹשׁ תְּקִיעוֹת: תְּקִיעָה תְּרוּעָה תְּקִיעָה. גָּמְרוּ לְהַקְרִיב, פּוֹתְחִין הָעֲזָרָה. יָצְאָה כַּת רִאשׁוֹנָה, נִכְנְסָה כַּת שְׁנִיָּה, נוֹעֲלִין דַּלְתוֹת הָעֲזָרָה. גָּמְרוּ, פּוֹתְחִין, יָצְאָה כַּת שְׁנִיָּה, נִכְנְסָה כַּת שְׁלִישִׁית, וּמַעֲשֵׂה כֻּלָּן שָׁוִין. וְאַחַר שֶׁיָּצְאוּ כֻּלָּן רוֹחֲצִין הָעֲזָרָה, וַאֲפִילוּ בְּשַׁבָּת, מִפְּנֵי לִכְלוּךְ הַדָּם שֶׁהָיָה בָהּ. וְכֵיצַד הָיְתָה הָרְחִיצָה? אַמַּת הַמַּיִם הָיְתָה עוֹבֶרֶת בַּעֲזָרָה, וְהָיָה לָהּ מָקוֹם לָצֵאת מִמֶּנָּה, וּכְשֶׁרוֹצִין לְהָדִיחַ אֶת הָרִצְפָּה, סוֹתְמִין מְקוֹם יְצִיאָתָהּ, וְהִיא מִתְמַלֵּאת עַל כָּל גְּדוֹתֶיהָ מִפֹּה וּמִפֹּה, עַד שֶׁהַמַּיִם עוֹלִים וְצָפִים מִכָּאן וּמִכָּאן, וּמְקַבֵּץ אֵלֶיהָ כָּל דָּם וְכָל לִכְלוּךְ שֶׁהָיָה בַּעֲזָרָה. וְאַחַר כָּךְ פּוֹתְחִין מְקוֹם יְצִיאָתָהּ, וְהַכֹּל יוֹצֵא עַד שֶׁנִּשְׁאָר הָרִצְפָּה מְנֻקָּה וּמְשֻׁפָּה. זֶהוּ כְּבוֹד הַבַּיִת. וְאִם הַפֶּסַח נִמְצָא טְרֵפָה, לֹא עָלָה לוֹ עַד שֶׁמֵּבִיא אַחֵר:

This is a very brief description of the order of the Pesach offering. The God-fearing person should recite it in its proper time, so that its recital should be regarded in place of its offering. One should be troubled about the destruction of the Beit Hamikdash, and plead before God, the Creator of the universe, that He rebuild it speedily in our days, Amen.

the Temple mount, the second group sits in the *chel* [an area just outside the Temple court], and the third stands in its place [in the courtyard]. After nightfall they go to their places and roast their Pesach offering. The Pesach offering was slaughtered in three groups, each group consisting of no less than thirty men. The first group entered, filling the Temple court. They closed [its doors], and while they were slaughtering it and offering its parts on the altar, they [the Levi'im] recited the Hallel. If they finished [Hallel] before all had sacrificed, they repeated it, and if they repeated it [and were not finished yet], they recited it a third time. Each time Hallel was recited, [the Kohanim] sounded three blasts of the trumpet: *tekiah, teruah, tekiah.* When the offering was ended, they opened the doors of the Temple court, the first group went out and the second entered, and they closed the doors of the Temple court. When they finished, they opened the doors, the second group went out and the third entered. The procedure of each group was the same. After they all had left, they washed the Temple court, even on Shabbat, of the dirt of the blood. How was the washing done? A water duct passed through the Temple court and had an outlet from the court. When they wished to wash the floor, they shut the outlet and the stream overflowed its sides until the water rose and flooded the [floor] all around and all the blood and dirt of the court were gathered to it. Then they opened the outlet, everything flowed out and the floor was completely clean; this is the honor of the Temple. If the Pesach offering was found to be unfit, one did not fulfill his obligation until he brings another one.

This is a very brief description of the order of the Pesach offering. The God-fearing person should recite it in its proper time, so that its recital should be regarded in place of its offering. One should be troubled about the destruction of the Beit Hamikdash, and plead before God, the Creator of the universe, that He rebuild it speedily in our days, Amen.

עֵרוּב תַּבְשִׁילִין

When the first two days of Pesach occur on Thursday and Friday, then on Wednesday one should make an *eruv tavshilin*. This is done in order that one may prepare food on the festival for Shabbat. The *eruv tavshilin* is made by taking matzah designated for Shabbat, as well as a highly regarded cooked food such as meat or fish, and handing these over to another person through whom he grants a share in this *eruv* to the entire community.

The one making the *eruv* hands the food items to another person, and says:

אֲנִי מְזַכֶּה לְכָל מִי שֶׁרוֹצֶה לִזְכּוֹת וְלִסְמוֹךְ עַל עֵרוּב זֶה:

The one holding the food items raises them a *tefach* (approximately 3 inches) and then returns them to the one making the *eruv*, who recites the following:

בָּרוּךְ אַתָּה יְיָ, אֱלֹהֵינוּ מֶלֶךְ הָעוֹלָם, אֲשֶׁר קִדְּשָׁנוּ בְּמִצְוֹתָיו, וְצִוָּנוּ עַל מִצְוַת עֵרוּב:

בְּדֵין יְהֵא שָׁרֵא לָנָא לַאֲפוּיֵי וּלְבַשּׁוּלֵי וּלְאַטְמוּנֵי וּלְאַדְלוּקֵי שְׁרָגָא וּלְתַקָּנָא וּלְמֶעֱבַד כָּל צָרְכָנָא מִיּוֹמָא טָבָא לְשַׁבַּתָּא, לָנָא וּלְכָל יִשְׂרָאֵל הַדָּרִים בָּעִיר הַזֹּאת:

The *eruv* must be made with full awareness of the act. Therefore, one who does not understand the above Aramaic text must recite it in a language he does understand.

The food items are then put aside to be eaten on Shabbat.

הַדְלָקַת נֵרוֹת

The festival lights are kindled at least eighteen minutes before sunset. Married women light two candles and many add an additional candle for each child; girls light one candle. After lighting the candle(s), draw the hands three times around the lights and towards the face, then place them over the eyes and recite the appropriate blessing. It is customary to give charity before lighting the festival candles.

When the first night of Pesach occurs on Friday night, if one forgot to light the candles before sunset, they should not be lit at all.

Eruv Tavshilin

When the first two days of Pesach occur on Thursday and Friday, then on Wednesday one should make an *eruv tavshilin*. This is done in order that one may prepare food on the festival for Shabbat. The *eruv tavshilin* is made by taking matzah designated for Shabbat, as well as a highly regarded cooked food such as meat or fish, and handing these over to another person through whom he grants a share in this *eruv* to the entire community.

The one making the *eruv* hands the food items to another person, and says:

אני I hereby grant a share in this *eruv* to anyone who wishes to participate in it and to depend upon it.

The one holding the food items raises them a *tefach* (approximately 3 inches) and then returns them to the one making the *eruv*, who recites the following:

ברוך Blessed are You, GOD our God, King of the universe, who has sanctified us with His commandments, and commanded us concerning the mitzvah of *eruv*.

בדין Through this it shall be permissible for us to bake, to cook, to put away [a dish to preserve its heat], to kindle a light, and to prepare and do on the Festival all that is necessary for the Shabbat— for us and for all Israelites who dwell in this city.

The *eruv* must be made with full awareness of the act. Therefore, one who does not understand the above Aramaic text must recite it in a language he does understand.

The food items are then put aside to be eaten on Shabbat.

Blessings for Candle Lighting

The festival lights are kindled at least eighteen minutes before sunset. Married women light two candles and many add an additional candle for each child; girls light one candle. After lighting the candle(s), draw the hands three times around the lights and towards the face, then place them over the eyes and recite the appropriate blessing. It is customary to give charity before lighting the festival candles.

When the first night of Pesach occurs on Friday night, if one forgot to light the candles before sunset, they should not be lit at all.

On the second night of Pesach, or when the first night occurs on Saturday night, the lights are kindled after nightfall (approximately 45–60 minutes after sunset—consult a Jewish calendar for the specific time in your area) from a pre-existing flame.

On Friday evening, add the words in shaded parentheses.

בָּרוּךְ אַתָּה יְיָ, אֱלֹהֵינוּ מֶלֶךְ הָעוֹלָם, אֲשֶׁר קִדְּשָׁנוּ בְּמִצְוֹתָיו, וְצִוָּנוּ לְהַדְלִיק נֵר שֶׁל (שַׁבָּת וְשֶׁל) יוֹם טוֹב:

בָּרוּךְ אַתָּה יְיָ, אֱלֹהֵינוּ מֶלֶךְ הָעוֹלָם, שֶׁהֶחֱיָנוּ וְקִיְּמָנוּ וְהִגִּיעָנוּ לִזְמַן הַזֶּה:

תקוני שבת

When the first night of Pesach occurs on Friday night, recite the following quietly upon returning home from the synagogue:

שָׁלוֹם עֲלֵיכֶם מַלְאֲכֵי הַשָּׁרֵת מַלְאֲכֵי עֶלְיוֹן —Say three times
מִמֶּלֶךְ מַלְכֵי הַמְּלָכִים הַקָּדוֹשׁ בָּרוּךְ הוּא:

בּוֹאֲכֶם לְשָׁלוֹם מַלְאֲכֵי הַשָּׁלוֹם מַלְאֲכֵי עֶלְיוֹן —Say three times
מִמֶּלֶךְ מַלְכֵי הַמְּלָכִים הַקָּדוֹשׁ בָּרוּךְ הוּא:

בָּרְכוּנִי לְשָׁלוֹם מַלְאֲכֵי הַשָּׁלוֹם מַלְאֲכֵי עֶלְיוֹן —Say three times
מִמֶּלֶךְ מַלְכֵי הַמְּלָכִים הַקָּדוֹשׁ בָּרוּךְ הוּא:

צֵאתְכֶם לְשָׁלוֹם מַלְאֲכֵי הַשָּׁלוֹם מַלְאֲכֵי עֶלְיוֹן —Say three times
מִמֶּלֶךְ מַלְכֵי הַמְּלָכִים הַקָּדוֹשׁ בָּרוּךְ הוּא:

כִּי מַלְאָכָיו יְצַוֶּה לָּךְ, לִשְׁמָרְךָ בְּכָל דְּרָכֶיךָ:
יְיָ יִשְׁמָר צֵאתְךָ וּבוֹאֶךָ, מֵעַתָּה וְעַד עוֹלָם:

אֵשֶׁת חַיִל מִי יִמְצָא, וְרָחֹק מִפְּנִינִים מִכְרָהּ. בָּטַח בָּהּ לֵב בַּעְלָהּ, וְשָׁלָל לֹא יֶחְסָר. גְּמָלַתְהוּ טוֹב וְלֹא רָע, כָּל יְמֵי חַיֶּיהָ. דָּרְשָׁה צֶמֶר וּפִשְׁתִּים, וַתַּעַשׂ בְּחֵפֶץ כַּפֶּיהָ.

26

On the second night of Pesach, or when the first night occurs on Saturday night, the lights are kindled after nightfall (approximately 45–60 minutes after sunset—consult a Jewish calendar for the specific time in your area) from a pre-existing flame.

On Friday evening, add the words in shaded parentheses. Transliteration, page 109.

בָּרוּךְ Blessed are You, GOD our God, King of the universe, who has sanctified us with His commandments, and commanded us to kindle the (Shabbat and) Yom Tov light.

בָּרוּךְ Blessed are You, GOD our God, King of the universe, who has granted us life, sustained us and enabled us to reach this occasion.

Hymns for Friday Night

When the first night of Pesach occurs on Friday night, recite the following quietly upon returning home from the synagogue:

Say three times: שָׁלוֹם Peace unto you, ministering angels, messengers of the Most High, of the supreme King of kings, the Holy One, blessed be He.

Say three times: בּוֹאֲכֶם May your coming be in peace, angels of peace, messengers of the Most High, of the supreme King of kings, the Holy One, blessed be He.

Say three times: בָּרְכוּנִי Bless me with peace, angels of peace, messengers of the Most High, of the supreme King of kings, the Holy One, blessed be He.

Say three times: צֵאתְכֶם May your departure be in peace, angels of peace, messengers of the Most High, of the supreme King of kings, the Holy One, blessed be He.

כִּי For He will instruct His angels in your behalf, to guard you in all your ways. GOD will guard your going and your coming from now and for all time.

אֵשֶׁת Who can find a wife of excellence? Her value far exceeds that of gems. The heart of her husband trusts in her, he lacks no gain. She treats him with goodness, never with evil, all the days of her life. She seeks out wool and flax, and

הָיְתָה כָּאֲנִיּוֹת סוֹחֵר, מִמֶּרְחָק תָּבִיא לַחְמָהּ. וַתָּקָם בְּעוֹד
לַיְלָה, וַתִּתֵּן טֶרֶף לְבֵיתָהּ, וְחֹק לְנַעֲרֹתֶיהָ. זָמְמָה שָׂדֶה
וַתִּקָּחֵהוּ, מִפְּרִי כַפֶּיהָ נָטְעָה כָּרֶם. חָגְרָה בְעוֹז מָתְנֶיהָ,
וַתְּאַמֵּץ זְרוֹעֹתֶיהָ. טָעֲמָה כִּי טוֹב סַחְרָהּ, לֹא יִכְבֶּה בַלַּיְלָה
נֵרָהּ. יָדֶיהָ שִׁלְּחָה בַכִּישׁוֹר, וְכַפֶּיהָ תָּמְכוּ פָלֶךְ. כַּפָּהּ פָּרְשָׂה
לֶעָנִי, וְיָדֶיהָ שִׁלְּחָה לָאֶבְיוֹן. לֹא תִירָא לְבֵיתָהּ מִשָּׁלֶג, כִּי
כָל בֵּיתָהּ לָבֻשׁ שָׁנִים. מַרְבַדִּים עָשְׂתָה לָּהּ, שֵׁשׁ וְאַרְגָּמָן
לְבוּשָׁהּ. נוֹדָע בַּשְּׁעָרִים בַּעְלָהּ, בְּשִׁבְתּוֹ עִם זִקְנֵי אָרֶץ. סָדִין
עָשְׂתָה וַתִּמְכֹּר, וַחֲגוֹר נָתְנָה לַכְּנַעֲנִי. עוֹז וְהָדָר לְבוּשָׁהּ,
וַתִּשְׂחַק לְיוֹם אַחֲרוֹן. פִּיהָ פָּתְחָה בְחָכְמָה, וְתוֹרַת חֶסֶד עַל
לְשׁוֹנָהּ. צוֹפִיָּה הֲלִיכוֹת בֵּיתָהּ, וְלֶחֶם עַצְלוּת לֹא תֹאכֵל.
קָמוּ בָנֶיהָ וַיְאַשְּׁרוּהָ, בַּעְלָהּ וַיְהַלְלָהּ. רַבּוֹת בָּנוֹת עָשׂוּ חָיִל,
וְאַתְּ עָלִית עַל כֻּלָּנָה. שֶׁקֶר הַחֵן וְהֶבֶל הַיֹּפִי, אִשָּׁה יִרְאַת
יְיָ הִיא תִתְהַלָּל. תְּנוּ לָהּ מִפְּרִי יָדֶיהָ, וִיהַלְלוּהָ בַשְּׁעָרִים
מַעֲשֶׂיהָ:

מִזְמוֹר לְדָוִד, יְיָ רֹעִי לֹא אֶחְסָר. בִּנְאוֹת דֶּשֶׁא יַרְבִּיצֵנִי,
עַל מֵי מְנֻחוֹת יְנַהֲלֵנִי. נַפְשִׁי יְשׁוֹבֵב, יַנְחֵנִי
בְמַעְגְּלֵי צֶדֶק לְמַעַן שְׁמוֹ. גַּם כִּי אֵלֵךְ בְּגֵיא צַלְמָוֶת לֹא
אִירָא רָע, כִּי אַתָּה עִמָּדִי, שִׁבְטְךָ וּמִשְׁעַנְתֶּךָ הֵמָּה יְנַחֲמֻנִי.
תַּעֲרֹךְ לְפָנַי שֻׁלְחָן נֶגֶד צֹרְרָי, דִּשַּׁנְתָּ בַשֶּׁמֶן רֹאשִׁי, כּוֹסִי
רְוָיָה. אַךְ טוֹב וָחֶסֶד יִרְדְּפוּנִי כָּל יְמֵי חַיָּי, וְשַׁבְתִּי בְּבֵית יְיָ
לְאֹרֶךְ יָמִים:

דָּא הִיא סְעוּדָתָא דַּחֲקַל תַּפּוּחִין קַדִּישִׁין:

אַתְקִינוּ סְעוּדָתָא דִּמְהֵימְנוּתָא שְׁלֵמָתָא חֶדְוָתָא דְמַלְכָּא
קַדִּישָׁא. אַתְקִינוּ סְעוּדָתָא דְמַלְכָּא, דָּא הִיא
סְעוּדָתָא דַּחֲקַל תַּפּוּחִין קַדִּישִׁין, וּזְעֵיר אַנְפִּין וְעַתִּיקָא
קַדִּישָׁא אַתְיָן לְסַעֲדָא בַהֲדַהּ:

works willingly with her hands. She is like the merchant ships; she brings her food from afar. She rises while it is still night, gives food to her household, and sets out the tasks for her maids. She considers a field and buys it; from her earnings she plants a vineyard. She girds her loins with strength, and flexes her arms. She realizes that her enterprise is profitable; her lamp does not go out at night. She puts her hands on the spindle, and her palms grasp the distaff. She holds out her hand to the poor, and extends her hands to the destitute. She does not fear for her household in the frost, for her entire household is clothed [warmly] in scarlet. She makes her own tapestries; her garments are of fine linen and purple. Her husband is well-known at the gates, as he sits with the elders of the land. She makes linens and sells [them]; she provides the merchants with girdles. Strength and dignity are her garb, she looks smilingly toward the future. She opens her mouth with wisdom, and the teaching of kindness is on her tongue. She watches the conduct of her household, and does not eat the bread of idleness. Her children rise and acclaim her, her husband—and he praises her: Many daughters have done worthily, but you surpass them all. Charm is deceptive and beauty is naught; a God-fearing woman is the one to be praised. Give her praise for her accomplishments, and let her deeds laud her at the gates.

מזמור A Psalm by David. GOD is my shepherd, I shall lack nothing. He makes me lie down in green pastures; He leads me beside still waters. He revives my soul; He directs me in paths of righteousness for the sake of His Name. Even if I will walk in the valley of the shadow of death, I will fear no evil, for You are with me; Your rod and Your staff—they will comfort me. You will prepare a table for me before my enemies; You have anointed my head with oil; my cup is full. Only goodness and kindness shall follow me all the days of my life, and I shall dwell in the House of GOD for many long years.

דא This is the meal of the holy *Chakal Tapuchin*.

אתקינו Prepare the meal of perfect faith, which is the delight of the holy King; prepare the meal of the King. This is the meal of the holy *Chakal Tapuchin*, and *Z'eir Anpin* and the holy Ancient One come to join her in the meal.

The
Seder

Order of the Haggadah   סדר הגדה

יסדר על שולחנו קערה בג' מצות מונחים זה על זה, הישראל ועליו הלוי ועליו הכהן. ועליו לימין הזרוע, וכנגדו לשמאל הביצה, תחתיהם באמצע המרור, ותחת הזרוע החרוסת, וכנגדו תחת הביצה הכרפס, ותחת המרור החזרת שעושין כורך.

The Seder should begin soon after returning home from the synagogue, but not before nightfall. The table should be set before nightfall; the Ka'ara (Seder plate) is prepared after nightfall.

The Seder plate is organized in the following order:

1 **Matzah | מצה** The matzot are placed on a tray, separated by napkins (or cloth). The "Yisrael" matzah is placed on a napkin; above it the "Levi" matzah; above these the "Kohen" matzah. A napkin (or cloth) is then placed above the "Kohen" matzah.

2 **Zeroa | זרוע** A roasted fowl's neck bone is placed above the matzot, on the upper right side.

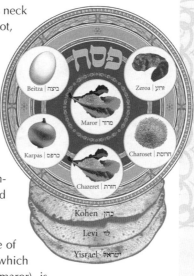

3 **Beitza | ביצה** A hard boiled egg is placed on the upper left side.

4 **Maror | מרור** A *kezayit* of bitter herbs is placed below these, in the center. It is customary to use romaine lettuce and horseradish for maror.

5 **Charoset | חרוסת** A mixture of apples, nuts, pears (and wine, which is added before eating the maror) is placed on the lower right side (beneath the zeroa).

6 **Karpas | כרפס** A raw onion or a boiled potato is placed on the lower left side (beneath the beitza).

7 **Chazeret | חזרת** A *kezayit* of bitter herbs is placed below these, in the center (beneath the maror). It is customary to use romaine lettuce and horseradish for chazeret.

32

Kadesh	Recite the Kiddush	קַדֵּשׁ
Urechatz	Wash the hands	וּרְחַץ
Karpas	Eat of the karpas	כַּרְפַּס
Yachatz	Break the middle matzah	יַחַץ
Maggid	Recite the Haggadah	מַגִּיד
Rachtzah	Wash the hands (for matzah)	רָחְצָה
Motzi	Recite the Hamotzi blessing	מוֹצִיא
Matzah	Recite the blessing for eating matzah	מַצָּה
Maror	Recite the blessing for eating maror	מָרוֹר
Korech	Eat the combination of matzah and maror	כּוֹרֵךְ
Shulchan Orech	Eat the festive meal	שֻׁלְחָן עוֹרֵךְ
Tzafun	Eat the hidden afikoman	צָפוּן
Berach	Recite the Blessing After Meals	בֵּרֵךְ
Hallel	Recite Hallel	הַלֵּל
Nirtzah	The Seder is accepted favorably	נִרְצָה

קַדֵּשׁ

English translation, pp. 36-37.

All present fill their cups for Kiddush.

אַתְקִינוּ סְעוּדָתָא דְּמַלְכָּא עִלָּאָה, דָּא הִיא סְעוּדָתָא דְּקוּדְשָׁא בְּרִיךְ הוּא וּשְׁכִינְתֵּיהּ:

All present stand for Kiddush.

Take the cup of wine in the right hand, pass it to the left hand, and lower it onto the palm of the right hand. The cup should be held three *tefachim* (approximately 9 in.) above the table throughout the Kiddush. (Note that this procedure is followed every time the cup is held throughout the Seder.)

Glance at the festival candles, then say:

On Friday night, begin here.

יוֹם הַשִּׁשִּׁי: וַיְכֻלּוּ הַשָּׁמַיִם וְהָאָרֶץ וְכָל צְבָאָם: וַיְכַל אֱלֹהִים בַּיּוֹם הַשְּׁבִיעִי מְלַאכְתּוֹ אֲשֶׁר עָשָׂה, וַיִּשְׁבֹּת בַּיּוֹם הַשְּׁבִיעִי מִכָּל מְלַאכְתּוֹ אֲשֶׁר עָשָׂה: וַיְבָרֶךְ אֱלֹהִים אֶת יוֹם הַשְּׁבִיעִי וַיְקַדֵּשׁ אֹתוֹ, כִּי בוֹ שָׁבַת מִכָּל מְלַאכְתּוֹ אֲשֶׁר בָּרָא אֱלֹהִים לַעֲשׂוֹת:

On weeknights, begin here.

Glance at the wine and say:

סַבְרִי מָרָנָן:

בָּרוּךְ אַתָּה יְיָ, אֱלֹהֵינוּ מֶלֶךְ הָעוֹלָם, בּוֹרֵא פְּרִי הַגָּפֶן:

On Friday night, add the words in shaded parentheses.

בָּרוּךְ אַתָּה יְיָ, אֱלֹהֵינוּ מֶלֶךְ הָעוֹלָם, אֲשֶׁר בָּחַר בָּנוּ מִכָּל עָם, וְרוֹמְמָנוּ מִכָּל לָשׁוֹן, וְקִדְּשָׁנוּ בְּמִצְוֹתָיו. וַתִּתֶּן לָנוּ יְיָ אֱלֹהֵינוּ בְּאַהֲבָה (שַׁבָּתוֹת לִמְנוּחָה וּ) מוֹעֲדִים לְשִׂמְחָה, חַגִּים וּזְמַנִּים לְשָׂשׂוֹן, אֶת יוֹם (הַשַּׁבָּת הַזֶּה וְאֶת יוֹם) חַג הַמַּצּוֹת הַזֶּה, וְאֶת יוֹם טוֹב

34

מִקְרָא קֹדֶשׁ הַזֶּה, זְמַן חֵרוּתֵנוּ, (בְּאַהֲבָה) מִקְרָא קֹדֶשׁ,
זֵכֶר לִיצִיאַת מִצְרָיִם. כִּי בָנוּ בָחַרְתָּ וְאוֹתָנוּ קִדַּשְׁתָּ מִכָּל
הָעַמִּים, (וְשַׁבָּת) וּמוֹעֲדֵי קָדְשֶׁךָ (בְּאַהֲבָה וּבְרָצוֹן) בְּשִׂמְחָה
וּבְשָׂשׂוֹן הִנְחַלְתָּנוּ: בָּרוּךְ אַתָּה יְיָ, מְקַדֵּשׁ (הַשַּׁבָּת
וְ) יִשְׂרָאֵל וְהַזְּמַנִּים:

On Saturday night, add the following.
Glance at the festival candles while reciting the following blessing:

בָּרוּךְ אַתָּה יְיָ, אֱלֹהֵינוּ מֶלֶךְ הָעוֹלָם, בּוֹרֵא מְאוֹרֵי הָאֵשׁ.

בָּרוּךְ אַתָּה יְיָ, אֱלֹהֵינוּ מֶלֶךְ הָעוֹלָם, הַמַּבְדִּיל בֵּין קֹדֶשׁ
לְחוֹל, בֵּין אוֹר לְחֹשֶׁךְ, בֵּין יִשְׂרָאֵל לָעַמִּים, בֵּין יוֹם
הַשְּׁבִיעִי לְשֵׁשֶׁת יְמֵי הַמַּעֲשֶׂה. בֵּין קְדֻשַּׁת שַׁבָּת לִקְדֻשַּׁת יוֹם
טוֹב הִבְדַּלְתָּ, וְאֶת יוֹם הַשְּׁבִיעִי מִשֵּׁשֶׁת יְמֵי הַמַּעֲשֶׂה קִדַּשְׁתָּ,
הִבְדַּלְתָּ וְקִדַּשְׁתָּ אֶת עַמְּךָ יִשְׂרָאֵל בִּקְדֻשָּׁתֶךָ: בָּרוּךְ אַתָּה יְיָ,
הַמַּבְדִּיל בֵּין קֹדֶשׁ לְקֹדֶשׁ:

One who has recited the שֶׁהֶחֱיָנוּ blessing during candle lighting should not recite it here.

בָּרוּךְ אַתָּה יְיָ, אֱלֹהֵינוּ מֶלֶךְ הָעוֹלָם, שֶׁהֶחֱיָנוּ וְקִיְּמָנוּ
וְהִגִּיעָנוּ לִזְמַן הַזֶּה: (אָמֵן —Listeners)

שׁוֹתֶה הַכּוֹס בִּישִׁיבָה בַּהֲסִבַּת שְׂמֹאל דֶּרֶךְ חֵרוּת:

Drink the entire cup without pause while seated, reclining on the left side as a sign of freedom. (One who cannot drink the entire cup should drink at least most of it.)

ורחץ

וּרְחַץ וְנוֹטֵל יָדָיו וְאֵינוֹ מְבָרֵךְ:

The hands are now washed in the following manner:

Pick up the cup containing the water in the right hand. Pass it to the left hand, and pour three times on the right hand. Then pass the cup to the right hand and pour three times on the left hand. It is customary to hold the cup with a towel when pouring on the left hand.

A little water from the final pouring should remain in the left hand, which is then rubbed over both hands together.

Dry the hands. The blessing עַל נְטִילַת יָדַיִם is not said.

Festival of holy convocation, the Season of our Freedom, (in love), a holy convocation, commemorating the
departure from Egypt. For You have chosen us and
sanctified us from all the nations, and You have given
us as a heritage Your holy (Shabbat and) Festivals, (in love
and favor,) in happiness and joy. Blessed are You, GOD,
who sanctifies (the Shabbat and) Israel and the festive
seasons.

On Saturday night, add the following.
Glance at the festival candles while reciting the following blessing:

ברוך Blessed are You, GOD, our God, King of the universe,
who creates the lights of the fire.

ברוך Blessed are You, GOD, our God, King of the universe,
who makes a distinction between sacred and profane, between light and darkness, between Israel and the nations,
between the seventh day and the six workdays. You have
made a distinction between the holiness of the Shabbat and
the holiness of the festival, and You have sanctified the
seventh day above the six workdays. You have set apart and
made holy Your people Israel with Your holiness. Blessed are
You, GOD, who makes a distinction between holy and holy.

One who has recited the blessing *Who has granted us life* during candle lighting
should not recite it here.

ברוך Blessed are You, GOD, our God, King of the
universe, who has granted us life, sustained us, and
enabled us to reach this occasion. (Listeners—Amen.)

Drink the entire cup without pause while seated, reclining on the left side as a sign
of freedom. (One who cannot drink the entire cup should drink at least most of it.)

Urechatz

The hands are now washed in the following manner:

Pick up the cup containing the water in the right hand. Pass it to the left hand,
and pour three times on the right hand. Then pass the cup to the right hand and
pour three times on the left hand. It is customary to hold the cup with a towel
when pouring on the left hand.

A little water from the final pouring should remain in the left hand, which is
then rubbed over both hands together.

Dry the hands. The blessing *concerning the washing of the hands* is not said.

Kadesh

All present fill their cups for Kiddush.

אתקינו Prepare the meal of the supernal King. This is the meal of the Holy One, blessed be He, and His Shechinah.

All present stand for Kiddush.

Take the cup of wine in the right hand, pass it to the left hand, and lower it onto the palm of the right hand. The cup should be held three *tefachim* (approximately 9 in.) above the table throughout the Kiddush. (Note that this procedure is followed every time the cup is held throughout the Seder.) Transliteration, page 108.

Glance at the festival candles, then say:

On Friday night, begin here.

יום The sixth day. And the heavens and the earth and all their hosts were completed. And on the seventh day God finished His work which He had made, and He rested on the seventh day from all His work which He had made. And God blessed the seventh day and made it holy, for on it He rested from all His work which God created to make.

On weeknights, begin here.

Glance at the wine and say:

סברי Attention, Gentlemen!

ברוך Blessed are You, GOD, our God, King of the universe, who creates the fruit of the vine.

On Friday night, add the words in shaded parentheses.

ברוך Blessed are You, GOD, our God, King of the universe, who has chosen us from among all people, and raised us above all tongues, and made us holy through His commandments. And You, GOD, our God, have given us in love (Shabbats for rest and) festivals for happiness, feasts and festive seasons for rejoicing, (this Shabbat day and) the day of this Feast of Matzot, and this

כרפס

נוטל פחות מכזית כרפס וטבול במי מלח או חומץ ויברך: **כרפס**

Take less than a *kezayit* of karpas, dip it into salt water or vinegar, and then recite the following blessing. When reciting the blessing, have in mind that it is also for the bitter herbs (of maror and korech) to be eaten later.

בָּרוּךְ אַתָּה יְיָ, אֱלֹהֵינוּ מֶלֶךְ הָעוֹלָם, בּוֹרֵא פְּרִי הָאֲדָמָה:

יכוין להוציא גם המרור בברכה זו:

The karpas is now eaten without reclining.

יחץ

ויקח מצה האמצעית ופורסה לשנים חלק אחד גדול מחבירו וחלק הגדול יניח לאפיקומן **יחץ**
והקטן מניח בין הב׳ מצות:

Break the middle matzah into two pieces (while still covered by the cloth), one larger than the other. The larger piece is broken into five pieces, and then wrapped in cloth and set aside to serve as afikoman. The smaller piece is put back between the two whole matzot.

מגיד

ומגביה הקערה שיש בה המצות ויאמר: **מגיד**

Uncover the matzot partially and say:

הָא לַחְמָא עַנְיָא דִי אֲכָלוּ אַבְהָתָנָא בְּאַרְעָא דְמִצְרָיִם. כָּל דִכְפִין יֵיתֵי וְיֵכוֹל, כָּל דִצְרִיךְ יֵיתֵי וְיִפְסַח. הַשַׁתָּא הָכָא, לְשָׁנָה הַבָּאָה בְּאַרְעָא דְיִשְׂרָאֵל. הַשַׁתָּא עַבְדִין, לְשָׁנָה הַבָּאָה בְּנֵי חוֹרִין:

The matzot are covered.

Take less than a *kezayit* of karpas, dip it into salt water or vinegar, and then recite the following blessing. When reciting the blessing, have in mind that it is also for the bitter herbs (of maror and korech) to be eaten later.

ברוך Blessed are You, GOD, our God, King of the universe, who creates the fruit of the earth.

The karpas is now eaten without reclining.

Break the middle matzah into two pieces (while still covered by the cloth), one larger than the other. The larger piece is broken into five pieces, and then wrapped in cloth and set aside to serve as afikoman. The smaller piece is put back between the two whole matzot.

Uncover the matzot partially and say:

הא This is the bread of affliction that our fathers ate in the land of Egypt. Whoever is hungry, let him come and eat; whoever is in need, let him come and conduct the [Seder of] Pesach. This year [we are] here; next year in the land of Israel. This year [we are] slaves; next year [we will be] free people.

The matzot are covered.

מסלקין הקערה עם המצות לצד אחר ומוזגין לו כוס ב' וכאן הבן שואל מה נשתנה:

The second cup is now poured, and the child asks מַה נִּשְׁתַּנָּה:
For the customary Yiddish version, see page 104.

מַה נִּשְׁתַּנָּה הַלַּיְלָה הַזֶּה מִכָּל הַלֵּילוֹת.

שֶׁבְּכָל הַלֵּילוֹת אֵין אָנוּ מַטְבִּילִין אֲפִילוּ פַּעַם אֶחָת הַלַּיְלָה הַזֶּה שְׁתֵּי פְּעָמִים:

שֶׁבְּכָל הַלֵּילוֹת אָנוּ אוֹכְלִין חָמֵץ אוֹ מַצָּה, הַלַּיְלָה הַזֶּה כֻּלּוֹ מַצָּה:

שֶׁבְּכָל הַלֵּילוֹת אָנוּ אוֹכְלִין שְׁאָר יְרָקוֹת, הַלַּיְלָה הַזֶּה מָרוֹר:

שֶׁבְּכָל הַלֵּילוֹת אָנוּ אוֹכְלִין בֵּין יוֹשְׁבִין וּבֵין מְסֻבִּין, הַלַּיְלָה הַזֶּה כֻּלָּנוּ מְסֻבִּין:

ומחזירין הקערה ומגלין מקצת הפת ואומרים עבדים וכו':

Uncover the matzot partially, and continue עֲבָדִים הָיִינוּ:

עֲבָדִים הָיִינוּ לְפַרְעֹה בְּמִצְרָיִם, וַיּוֹצִיאֵנוּ יְיָ אֱלֹהֵינוּ מִשָּׁם בְּיָד חֲזָקָה וּבִזְרֹעַ נְטוּיָה, וְאִלּוּ לֹא הוֹצִיא הַקָּדוֹשׁ בָּרוּךְ הוּא אֶת אֲבוֹתֵינוּ מִמִּצְרַיִם, הֲרֵי אָנוּ וּבָנֵינוּ וּבְנֵי בָנֵינוּ מְשֻׁעְבָּדִים הָיִינוּ לְפַרְעֹה בְּמִצְרָיִם. וַאֲפִילוּ כֻּלָּנוּ חֲכָמִים כֻּלָּנוּ נְבוֹנִים כֻּלָּנוּ יוֹדְעִים אֶת הַתּוֹרָה, מִצְוָה עָלֵינוּ לְסַפֵּר בִּיצִיאַת מִצְרָיִם, וְכָל הַמַּרְבֶּה לְסַפֵּר בִּיצִיאַת מִצְרַיִם הֲרֵי זֶה מְשֻׁבָּח:

מַעֲשֶׂה בְּרַבִּי אֱלִיעֶזֶר וְרַבִּי יְהוֹשֻׁעַ וְרַבִּי אֶלְעָזָר בֶּן עֲזַרְיָה וְרַבִּי עֲקִיבָא וְרַבִּי טַרְפוֹן, שֶׁהָיוּ מְסֻבִּים בִּבְנֵי בְרַק, וְהָיוּ מְסַפְּרִים בִּיצִיאַת מִצְרַיִם כָּל

The second cup is now poured, and the child asks *What makes this night different*: Transliteration, page 108.

מה What makes this night different from all [other] nights?

On all nights we need not dip even once, and on this night we do so twice!

On all nights we eat chametz or matzah, and on this night, only matzah!

On all nights we eat any kind of vegetables, and on this night, maror!

On all nights we eat sitting upright or reclining, and on this night we all recline!

Uncover the matzot partially, and continue *We were slaves...*:

עבדים We were slaves to Pharaoh in Egypt, and GOD, our God, took us out from there with a strong hand and with an outstretched arm. If the Holy One, blessed be He, had not taken our fathers out of Egypt, then we, our children and our children's children would have remained enslaved to Pharaoh in Egypt. Even if all of us were wise, all of us understanding, all of us knowing the Torah, we would still be obligated to discuss the exodus from Egypt; and everyone who discusses the exodus from Egypt at length is praiseworthy.

מעשה It happened that Rabbi Eliezer, Rabbi Yehoshua, Rabbi Elazar ben Azaryah, Rabbi Akiva and Rabbi Tarphon were reclining [at a Seder] in B'nei Berak. They were discussing the exodus from Egypt all that night, until their students came and

אוֹתוֹ הַלַּיְלָה, עַד שֶׁבָּאוּ תַלְמִידֵיהֶם וְאָמְרוּ לָהֶם:
רַבּוֹתֵינוּ, הִגִּיעַ זְמַן קְרִיאַת שְׁמַע שֶׁל שַׁחֲרִית:

אָמַר רַבִּי אֶלְעָזָר בֶּן עֲזַרְיָה: הֲרֵי אֲנִי כְּבֶן שִׁבְעִים
שָׁנָה, וְלֹא זָכִיתִי שֶׁתֵּאָמֵר יְצִיאַת מִצְרַיִם
בַּלֵּילוֹת, עַד שֶׁדְּרָשָׁהּ בֶּן זוֹמָא, שֶׁנֶּאֱמַר: לְמַעַן תִּזְכֹּר
אֶת יוֹם צֵאתְךָ מֵאֶרֶץ מִצְרַיִם כֹּל יְמֵי חַיֶּיךָ. יְמֵי חַיֶּיךָ
הַיָּמִים, כֹּל יְמֵי חַיֶּיךָ לְהָבִיא הַלֵּילוֹת. וַחֲכָמִים
אוֹמְרִים: יְמֵי חַיֶּיךָ הָעוֹלָם הַזֶּה, כֹּל יְמֵי חַיֶּיךָ לְהָבִיא
לִימוֹת הַמָּשִׁיחַ:

בָּרוּךְ הַמָּקוֹם, בָּרוּךְ הוּא, בָּרוּךְ שֶׁנָּתַן תּוֹרָה לְעַמּוֹ
יִשְׂרָאֵל, בָּרוּךְ הוּא, כְּנֶגֶד אַרְבָּעָה בָנִים
דִּבְּרָה תוֹרָה: אֶחָד חָכָם, וְאֶחָד רָשָׁע, וְאֶחָד תָּם,
וְאֶחָד שֶׁאֵינוֹ יוֹדֵעַ לִשְׁאוֹל:

חָכָם מַה הוּא אוֹמֵר: מָה הָעֵדֹת וְהַחֻקִּים
וְהַמִּשְׁפָּטִים אֲשֶׁר צִוָּה יְיָ אֱלֹהֵינוּ אֶתְכֶם.
וְאַף אַתָּה אֱמוֹר לוֹ כְּהִלְכוֹת הַפֶּסַח, אֵין מַפְטִירִין
אַחַר הַפֶּסַח אֲפִיקוֹמָן:

רָשָׁע מַה הוּא אוֹמֵר: מָה הָעֲבֹדָה הַזֹּאת לָכֶם.
לָכֶם וְלֹא לוֹ, וּלְפִי שֶׁהוֹצִיא אֶת עַצְמוֹ מִן
הַכְּלָל, כָּפַר בְּעִקָּר. וְאַף אַתָּה הַקְהֵה אֶת שִׁנָּיו וֶאֱמָר
לוֹ: בַּעֲבוּר זֶה עָשָׂה יְיָ לִי בְּצֵאתִי מִמִּצְרַיִם, לִי וְלֹא
לוֹ, אִלּוּ הָיָה שָׁם לֹא הָיָה נִגְאָל:

תָּם מַה הוּא אוֹמֵר: מַה זֹּאת, וְאָמַרְתָּ אֵלָיו: בְּחֹזֶק
יָד הוֹצִיאָנוּ יְיָ מִמִּצְרַיִם מִבֵּית עֲבָדִים:

told them: "Our Masters! The time has come for reciting the morning Shema!"

אמר Rabbi Elazar ben Azaryah said: "I am like a man of seventy years old, yet I did not succeed in proving that the exodus from Egypt must be mentioned at night—until Ben Zoma explained it: 'It is said, "That you may remember the day you left Egypt all the days of your life"; now "the days of your life" refers to the days, [and the additional word] "all" indicates the inclusion of the nights!'" The Sages, however, said: "'The days of your life' refers to the present-day world; and 'all' indicates the inclusion of the days of Moshiach."

ברוך Blessed is the Omnipresent One, blessed be He! Blessed is He who gave the Torah to His people Israel, blessed be He! The Torah speaks of four children: One is wise, one is wicked, one is simple and one does not know how to ask.

חכם The wise one, what does he say? "What are the testimonies, the statutes and the laws which GOD, our God, has commanded you?" You, in turn, shall instruct him in the laws of Pesach, [up to] "one is not to eat any dessert after the Pesach-lamb."

רשע The wicked one, what does he say? "What is this service to you?!" He says "to you," but not to him! By thus excluding himself from the community he has denied that which is fundamental. You, therefore, blunt his teeth and say to him: "'It is because of this that GOD acted for me when I left Egypt'; 'for me'—but not for him! If he had been there, he would not have been redeemed!"

תם The simpleton, what does he say? "What is this?" Thus you shall say to him: "GOD took us out of Egypt, from the house of slaves, with a strong hand."

וְשֶׁאֵינוֹ יוֹדֵעַ לִשְׁאוֹל, אַתְּ פְּתַח לוֹ, שֶׁנֶּאֱמַר:
וְהִגַּדְתָּ לְבִנְךָ בַּיּוֹם הַהוּא לֵאמֹר: בַּעֲבוּר
זֶה עָשָׂה יְיָ לִי בְּצֵאתִי מִמִּצְרָיִם:

יָכוֹל מֵרֹאשׁ חֹדֶשׁ, תַּלְמוּד לוֹמַר: בַּיּוֹם הַהוּא. אִי
בַּיּוֹם הַהוּא, יָכוֹל מִבְּעוֹד יוֹם, תַּלְמוּד לוֹמַר:
בַּעֲבוּר זֶה, בַּעֲבוּר זֶה לֹא אָמַרְתִּי אֶלָּא בְּשָׁעָה שֶׁיֵּשׁ
מַצָּה וּמָרוֹר מֻנָּחִים לְפָנֶיךָ:

מִתְּחִלָּה עוֹבְדֵי עֲבוֹדָה זָרָה הָיוּ אֲבוֹתֵינוּ, וְעַכְשָׁו
קֵרְבָנוּ הַמָּקוֹם לַעֲבֹדָתוֹ, שֶׁנֶּאֱמַר: וַיֹּאמֶר
יְהוֹשֻׁעַ אֶל כָּל הָעָם, כֹּה אָמַר יְיָ אֱלֹהֵי יִשְׂרָאֵל:
בְּעֵבֶר הַנָּהָר יָשְׁבוּ אֲבוֹתֵיכֶם מֵעוֹלָם, תֶּרַח אֲבִי
אַבְרָהָם וַאֲבִי נָחוֹר, וַיַּעַבְדוּ אֱלֹהִים אֲחֵרִים:

וָאֶקַּח אֶת אֲבִיכֶם אֶת אַבְרָהָם מֵעֵבֶר הַנָּהָר,
וָאוֹלֵךְ אוֹתוֹ בְּכָל אֶרֶץ כְּנָעַן, וָאַרְבֶּה אֶת
זַרְעוֹ וָאֶתֶּן לוֹ אֶת יִצְחָק: וָאֶתֵּן לְיִצְחָק אֶת יַעֲקֹב
וְאֶת עֵשָׂו, וָאֶתֵּן לְעֵשָׂו אֶת הַר שֵׂעִיר לָרֶשֶׁת אוֹתוֹ,
וְיַעֲקֹב וּבָנָיו יָרְדוּ מִצְרָיִם:

בָּרוּךְ שׁוֹמֵר הַבְטָחָתוֹ לְיִשְׂרָאֵל, בָּרוּךְ הוּא,
שֶׁהַקָּדוֹשׁ בָּרוּךְ הוּא חִשַּׁב אֶת הַקֵּץ
לַעֲשׂוֹת כְּמָה שֶׁאָמַר לְאַבְרָהָם אָבִינוּ בִּבְרִית בֵּין
הַבְּתָרִים, שֶׁנֶּאֱמַר: וַיֹּאמֶר לְאַבְרָם: יָדֹעַ תֵּדַע כִּי גֵר
יִהְיֶה זַרְעֲךָ בְּאֶרֶץ לֹא לָהֶם, וַעֲבָדוּם וְעִנּוּ אֹתָם,
אַרְבַּע מֵאוֹת שָׁנָה: וְגַם אֶת הַגּוֹי אֲשֶׁר יַעֲבֹדוּ דָן
אָנֹכִי, וְאַחֲרֵי כֵן יֵצְאוּ בִּרְכֻשׁ גָּדוֹל:

ושאינו As for the one who does not know how to ask, you must initiate him, as it is said: "You shall tell your child on that day, 'It is because of this that GOD acted for me when I left Egypt.'"

יכול One may think that [the discussion of the Exodus] must be from the first of the month. The Torah therefore says, "On that day." "On that day," however, could mean while it is yet daytime; the Torah therefore says, "It is because of this." The expression "because of this" can only be said when matzah and maror are placed before you.

מתחלה In the beginning our fathers served idols; but now the Omnipresent One has brought us close to His service, as it is said: "Joshua said to all the people: Thus said GOD, the God of Israel, 'Your fathers used to live on the other side of the river—Terach, the father of Abraham and the father of Nachor—and they served other gods.

ואקח "'And I took your father Abraham from beyond the river, and I led him throughout the whole land of Canaan. I increased his seed and gave him Isaac, and to Isaac I gave Jacob and Esau. To Esau I gave Mount Seir to possess it, and Jacob and his sons went down to Egypt.'"

ברוך Blessed is He who keeps His promise to Israel, blessed be He! For the Holy One, blessed be He, calculated the end [of the bondage], in order to do as He had said to our father Abraham at the Covenant between the Portions, as it is said: "And He said to Abraham, 'You shall know that your seed will be strangers in a land that is not theirs, and they will enslave them and make them suffer, for four hundred years. But I shall also judge the nation whom they shall serve, and after that they will come out with great wealth.'"

צריך להגביה הכוס ולכסות הפת כן כתב האר"י ז"ל:

According to the Arizal, the matzot are covered and the cup is then held in the palm
of the right hand for the following paragraph.

וְהִיא שֶׁעָמְדָה לַאֲבוֹתֵינוּ וְלָנוּ, שֶׁלֹּא אֶחָד
בִּלְבַד עָמַד עָלֵינוּ לְכַלּוֹתֵנוּ אֶלָּא שֶׁבְּכָל
דּוֹר וָדוֹר עוֹמְדִים עָלֵינוּ לְכַלּוֹתֵנוּ, וְהַקָּדוֹשׁ
בָּרוּךְ הוּא מַצִּילֵנוּ מִיָּדָם: יעמיד הכוס ויגלה הפת:

Place the cup on the table and uncover the matzot.

צֵא וּלְמַד מַה בִּקֵּשׁ לָבָן הָאֲרַמִּי לַעֲשׂוֹת לְיַעֲקֹב
אָבִינוּ, שֶׁפַּרְעֹה לֹא גָזַר אֶלָּא עַל הַזְּכָרִים,
וְלָבָן בִּקֵּשׁ לַעֲקוֹר אֶת הַכֹּל, שֶׁנֶּאֱמַר: אֲרַמִּי אֹבֵד
אָבִי, וַיֵּרֶד מִצְרַיְמָה וַיָּגָר שָׁם בִּמְתֵי מְעָט, וַיְהִי
שָׁם לְגוֹי גָּדוֹל עָצוּם וָרָב:

וַיֵּרֶד מִצְרַיְמָה, אָנוּס עַל פִּי הַדִּבּוּר:

וַיָּגָר שָׁם, מְלַמֵּד שֶׁלֹּא יָרַד יַעֲקֹב אָבִינוּ
לְהִשְׁתַּקֵּעַ בְּמִצְרַיִם אֶלָּא לָגוּר שָׁם, שֶׁנֶּאֱמַר: וַיֹּאמְרוּ
אֶל פַּרְעֹה לָגוּר בָּאָרֶץ בָּאנוּ, כִּי אֵין מִרְעֶה לַצֹּאן
אֲשֶׁר לַעֲבָדֶיךָ, כִּי כָבֵד הָרָעָב בְּאֶרֶץ כְּנָעַן, וְעַתָּה
יֵשְׁבוּ נָא עֲבָדֶיךָ בְּאֶרֶץ גֹּשֶׁן:

בִּמְתֵי מְעָט, כְּמָה שֶׁנֶּאֱמַר: בְּשִׁבְעִים נֶפֶשׁ יָרְדוּ
אֲבֹתֶיךָ מִצְרַיְמָה, וְעַתָּה שָׂמְךָ יְיָ אֱלֹהֶיךָ כְּכוֹכְבֵי
הַשָּׁמַיִם לָרֹב:

וַיְהִי שָׁם לְגוֹי, מְלַמֵּד שֶׁהָיוּ יִשְׂרָאֵל מְצֻיָּנִים שָׁם:

גָּדוֹל עָצוּם, כְּמָה שֶׁנֶּאֱמַר: וּבְנֵי יִשְׂרָאֵל פָּרוּ

According to the Arizal, the matzot are covered and the cup is then held in the palm of the right hand for the following paragraph. Transliteration, page 109.

וְהִיא This is what has stood by our fathers and us! For not just one alone has risen against us to destroy us, but in every generation they rise against us to destroy us; and the Holy One, blessed be He, saves us from their hand!

Place the cup on the table and uncover the matzot.

צֵא Go forth and learn what Laban the Aramean wanted to do to our father Jacob. Pharaoh had issued a decree against the male children only, but Laban wanted to uproot everyone—as it is said: **"The Aramean wished to destroy my father; and he went down to Egypt and sojourned there, few in number; and he became there a nation—great, mighty and numerous."**

"And he went down to Egypt"—forced by Divine decree.

"And he sojourned there"—this teaches that our father Jacob did not go down to Egypt to settle, but only to live there temporarily. Thus it is said, "They said to Pharaoh, 'We have come to sojourn in the land, for there is no pasture for your servants' flocks because the hunger is severe in the land of Canaan; and now, please, let your servants dwell in the land of Goshen.'"

"Few in number"—as it is said: "Your fathers went down to Egypt with seventy persons, and now, GOD, your God, has made you as numerous as the stars of heaven."

"And he became there a nation"—this teaches that Israel was distinctive there.

"Great, mighty"—as it is said: "And the children

וַיִּשְׁרְצוּ וַיִּרְבּוּ וַיַּעַצְמוּ בִּמְאֹד מְאֹד וַתִּמָּלֵא הָאָרֶץ
אֹתָם:

וָרָב, כְּמָה שֶׁנֶּאֱמַר: וָאֶעֱבֹר עָלַיִךְ וָאֶרְאֵךְ
מִתְבּוֹסֶסֶת בְּדָמָיִךְ, וָאֹמַר לָךְ בְּדָמַיִךְ חֲיִי, וָאֹמַר לָךְ
בְּדָמַיִךְ חֲיִי: רְבָבָה כְּצֶמַח הַשָּׂדֶה נְתַתִּיךְ, וַתִּרְבִּי
וַתִּגְדְּלִי וַתָּבֹאִי בַּעֲדִי עֲדָיִים, שָׁדַיִם נָכֹנוּ וּשְׂעָרֵךְ
צִמֵּחַ, וְאַתְּ עֵרֹם וְעֶרְיָה:

וַיָּרֵעוּ אֹתָנוּ הַמִּצְרִים וַיְעַנּוּנוּ, וַיִּתְּנוּ עָלֵינוּ עֲבֹדָה
קָשָׁה:

וַיָּרֵעוּ אֹתָנוּ הַמִּצְרִים, כְּמָה שֶׁנֶּאֱמַר: הָבָה
נִתְחַכְּמָה לוֹ, פֶּן יִרְבֶּה, וְהָיָה כִּי תִקְרֶאנָה מִלְחָמָה,
וְנוֹסַף גַּם הוּא עַל שֹׂנְאֵינוּ, וְנִלְחַם בָּנוּ וְעָלָה מִן
הָאָרֶץ:

וַיְעַנּוּנוּ, כְּמָה שֶׁנֶּאֱמַר: וַיָּשִׂימוּ עָלָיו שָׂרֵי מִסִּים
לְמַעַן עַנֹּתוֹ בְּסִבְלֹתָם, וַיִּבֶן עָרֵי מִסְכְּנוֹת לְפַרְעֹה, אֶת
פִּתֹם וְאֶת רַעַמְסֵס:

וַיִּתְּנוּ עָלֵינוּ עֲבֹדָה קָשָׁה, כְּמָה שֶׁנֶּאֱמַר: וַיַּעֲבִדוּ
מִצְרַיִם אֶת בְּנֵי יִשְׂרָאֵל בְּפָרֶךְ: וַיְמָרְרוּ אֶת חַיֵּיהֶם
בַּעֲבֹדָה קָשָׁה בְּחֹמֶר וּבִלְבֵנִים וּבְכָל עֲבֹדָה בַּשָּׂדֶה,
אֵת כָּל עֲבֹדָתָם אֲשֶׁר עָבְדוּ בָהֶם בְּפָרֶךְ:

וַנִּצְעַק אֶל יְיָ אֱלֹהֵי אֲבֹתֵינוּ, וַיִּשְׁמַע יְיָ אֶת
קֹלֵנוּ, וַיַּרְא אֶת עָנְיֵנוּ וְאֶת עֲמָלֵנוּ וְאֶת
לַחֲצֵנוּ:

of Israel were fruitful and increased abundantly, and multiplied and became very, very mighty, and the land became filled with them."

"And numerous"—as it is said: "I passed over you and saw you wallowing in your bloods, and I said to you, 'By your blood you shall live,' and I said to you, 'By your blood you shall live!' I caused you to thrive like the plants of the field, and you increased and grew and became very beautiful, your bosom fashioned and your hair grown long, but you were naked and bare."

ויֵרֵעוּ "The Egyptians treated us badly and they made us suffer, and they put hard work upon us."

"The Egyptians treated us badly"—as it is said: "Come, let us act cunningly with [the people] lest they multiply and, if there should be a war against us, they will join our enemies, fight against us and leave the land."

"And they made us suffer"—as it is said: "They set taskmasters over [the people of Israel] to make them suffer with their burdens, and they built storage cities for Pharaoh, Pitom and Raamses."

"And they put hard work upon us"—as it is said: "The Egyptians made the children of Israel work with rigor. And they made their lives bitter with hard work, with mortar and with bricks, and with all manner of service in the field; all their work which they made them perform with rigor."

וַנִּצְעַק "And we cried out to GOD, the God of our fathers, and GOD heard our voice and saw our suffering, our labor and our oppression."

וַנִּצְעַק אֶל יְיָ אֱלֹהֵי אֲבֹתֵינוּ, כְּמָה שֶׁנֶּאֱמַר:
וַיְהִי בַיָּמִים הָרַבִּים הָהֵם וַיָּמָת מֶלֶךְ מִצְרַיִם, וַיֵּאָנְחוּ
בְנֵי יִשְׂרָאֵל מִן הָעֲבֹדָה וַיִּזְעָקוּ, וַתַּעַל שַׁוְעָתָם אֶל
הָאֱלֹהִים מִן הָעֲבֹדָה:

וַיִּשְׁמַע יְיָ אֶת קֹלֵנוּ, כְּמָה שֶׁנֶּאֱמַר: וַיִּשְׁמַע
אֱלֹהִים אֶת נַאֲקָתָם, וַיִּזְכֹּר אֱלֹהִים אֶת בְּרִיתוֹ אֶת
אַבְרָהָם אֶת יִצְחָק וְאֶת יַעֲקֹב:

וַיַּרְא אֶת עָנְיֵנוּ, זוֹ פְּרִישׁוּת דֶּרֶךְ אֶרֶץ, כְּמָה
שֶׁנֶּאֱמַר: וַיַּרְא אֱלֹהִים אֶת בְּנֵי יִשְׂרָאֵל, וַיֵּדַע אֱלֹהִים:

וְאֶת עֲמָלֵנוּ, אֵלּוּ הַבָּנִים, כְּמָה שֶׁנֶּאֱמַר: כָּל הַבֵּן
הַיִּלּוֹד הַיְאֹרָה תַּשְׁלִיכֻהוּ, וְכָל הַבַּת תְּחַיּוּן:

וְאֶת לַחֲצֵנוּ, זֶה הַדְּחַק, כְּמָה שֶׁנֶּאֱמַר: וְגַם
רָאִיתִי אֶת הַלַּחַץ אֲשֶׁר מִצְרַיִם לֹחֲצִים אֹתָם:

וַיּוֹצִיאֵנוּ יְיָ מִמִּצְרַיִם בְּיָד חֲזָקָה וּבִזְרֹעַ נְטוּיָה
וּבְמֹרָא גָּדֹל וּבְאֹתוֹת וּבְמֹפְתִים:

וַיּוֹצִיאֵנוּ יְיָ מִמִּצְרַיִם, לֹא עַל יְדֵי מַלְאָךְ וְלֹא
עַל יְדֵי שָׂרָף וְלֹא עַל יְדֵי שָׁלִיחַ, אֶלָּא הַקָּדוֹשׁ בָּרוּךְ
הוּא בִּכְבוֹדוֹ וּבְעַצְמוֹ, שֶׁנֶּאֱמַר: וְעָבַרְתִּי בְאֶרֶץ
מִצְרַיִם בַּלַּיְלָה הַזֶּה, וְהִכֵּיתִי כָל בְּכוֹר בְּאֶרֶץ מִצְרַיִם
מֵאָדָם וְעַד בְּהֵמָה, וּבְכָל אֱלֹהֵי מִצְרַיִם אֶעֱשֶׂה
שְׁפָטִים, אֲנִי יְיָ: וְעָבַרְתִּי בְאֶרֶץ מִצְרַיִם, אֲנִי וְלֹא
מַלְאָךְ. וְהִכֵּיתִי כָל בְּכוֹר בְּאֶרֶץ מִצְרַיִם, אֲנִי וְלֹא
שָׂרָף. וּבְכָל אֱלֹהֵי מִצְרַיִם אֶעֱשֶׂה שְׁפָטִים, אֲנִי וְלֹא
הַשָּׁלִיחַ. אֲנִי יְיָ, אֲנִי הוּא וְלֹא אַחֵר:

"**And we cried out to GOD, the God of our fathers**"—as it is said: "During that long period, the king of Egypt died; and the children of Israel groaned because of the servitude, and they cried out. and their cry for help from their servitude rose up to God."

"**And GOD heard our voice**"—as it is said: "And God heard their groaning, and God remembered His covenant with Abraham, Isaac and Jacob."

"**And He saw our suffering**"—this refers to the separation of husband and wife, as it is said: "God saw the children of Israel, and God took note."

"**Our labor**"—this refers to the children, as it is said: "Every boy that is born you shall throw into the river, and every girl you shall keep alive."

"**And our oppression**"—this refers to the pressure, as it is said: "I have seen the oppression with which the Egyptians oppress them."

ויוציאנו "**GOD took us out of Egypt with a strong hand and an outstretched arm, and with a great manifestation, and with signs and wonders.**"

"**GOD took us out of Egypt**"—not through an angel, not through a *seraph* and not through a messenger. The Holy One, blessed be He, did it in His glory by Himself! Thus it is said: "On that night I will pass through the land of Egypt, and I will smite every first-born in the land of Egypt, from man to beast, and I will carry out judgments against all the gods of Egypt, I—GOD." "I will pass through the land of Egypt," I and not an angel. "And I will smite every first-born in the land of Egypt," I and not a *seraph*. "And I will carry out judgments against all the gods of Egypt," I and not a messenger. "I—GOD," it is I, and none other!

בְּיָד חֲזָקָה, זֶה הַדֶּבֶר, כְּמָה שֶׁנֶּאֱמַר: הִנֵּה יַד יְיָ
הוֹיָה בְּמִקְנְךָ אֲשֶׁר בַּשָּׂדֶה, בַּסּוּסִים בַּחֲמֹרִים
בַּגְּמַלִּים בַּבָּקָר וּבַצֹּאן, דֶּבֶר כָּבֵד מְאֹד:

וּבִזְרֹעַ נְטוּיָה, זוֹ הַחֶרֶב, כְּמָה שֶׁנֶּאֱמַר: וְחַרְבּוֹ
שְׁלוּפָה בְּיָדוֹ נְטוּיָה עַל יְרוּשָׁלָיִם:

וּבְמֹרָא גָּדֹל, זֶה גִּלּוּי שְׁכִינָה, כְּמָה שֶׁנֶּאֱמַר: אוֹ
הֲנִסָּה אֱלֹהִים לָבוֹא לָקַחַת לוֹ גוֹי מִקֶּרֶב גּוֹי בְּמַסֹּת
בְּאֹתֹת וּבְמוֹפְתִים וּבְמִלְחָמָה וּבְיָד חֲזָקָה וּבִזְרֹעַ
נְטוּיָה וּבְמוֹרָאִים גְּדֹלִים, כְּכֹל אֲשֶׁר עָשָׂה לָכֶם יְיָ
אֱלֹהֵיכֶם בְּמִצְרַיִם לְעֵינֶיךָ:

וּבְאֹתוֹת, זֶה הַמַּטֶּה, כְּמָה שֶׁנֶּאֱמַר: וְאֶת הַמַּטֶּה
הַזֶּה תִּקַּח בְּיָדֶךָ, אֲשֶׁר תַּעֲשֶׂה בּוֹ אֶת הָאֹתֹת:

וּבְמוֹפְתִים, זֶה הַדָּם, כְּמָה שֶׁנֶּאֱמַר: וְנָתַתִּי
מוֹפְתִים בַּשָּׁמַיִם וּבָאָרֶץ—

באמירת דם ואש ותמרות עשן ישפוך ג' שפיכות ואין ליטול באצבע לשפוך כ"א בכוס עצמו
וישפוך לתוך כלי שבור (ויכוין שהכוס הוא סוד המלכות ושופך מהיין שבתוכו סוד האף והזעם
שבה ע"י כח הבינה לתוך כלי שבור סוד הקליפה שנקראת ארור):

While saying each of the following three "wonders"—דָּם, וָאֵשׁ, וְתִימְרוֹת עָשָׁן—spill a
drop of wine from the cup, into a broken dish. Do not remove wine by dipping in a
finger, but by spilling from the cup itself. (Have in mind that the spilled wine
represents the punishments mentioned here. The wine remaining in the cup,
however, becomes "wine that causes joy.")

דָּם וָאֵשׁ וְתִימְרוֹת עָשָׁן:

דָּבָר אַחֵר: בְּיָד חֲזָקָה שְׁתַּיִם, וּבִזְרֹעַ נְטוּיָה שְׁתַּיִם,
וּבְמֹרָא גָּדֹל שְׁתַּיִם, וּבְאֹתוֹת שְׁתַּיִם,
וּבְמוֹפְתִים שְׁתַּיִם:

"With a strong hand"—this refers to the pestilence, as it is said: "Behold, the hand of GOD will be upon your livestock in the field, upon the horses, the donkeys, the camels, the herds and the flocks, a very severe pestilence."

"And with an outstretched arm"—this refers to the sword, as it is said: "His sword was drawn in his hand, stretched out over Jerusalem."

"And with a great manifestation"—this refers to the revelation of the *Shechinah* (Divine Presence), as it is said: "Has any god ever tried to take for himself a nation from the midst of another nation, with trials, signs and wonders, with war and with a strong hand and an outstretched arm, and with great manifestations, like all that GOD, your God, did for you in Egypt before your eyes!"

"And with signs"—this refers to the staff, as it is said: "Take into your hand this staff, with which you shall perform the signs."

"And wonders"—this refers to the blood, as it is said: "And I shall show wonders in heaven and on earth—

While saying each of the following three "wonders"—*Blood, fire, and pillars of smoke*—spill a drop of wine from the cup, into a broken dish. Do not remove wine by dipping in a finger, but by spilling from the cup itself. (Have in mind that the spilled wine represents the punishments mentioned here. The wine remaining in the cup, however, becomes "wine that causes joy.")

דם Blood, and fire and pillars of smoke."

דבר Another explanation: "Strong hand" indicates two [plagues]; "Outstretched arm," another two; "Great manifestation," another two; "Signs," another two; and "Wonders," another two.

אֵלּוּ עֶשֶׂר מַכּוֹת שֶׁהֵבִיא הַקָּדוֹשׁ בָּרוּךְ הוּא עַל הַמִּצְרִים בְּמִצְרַיִם, וְאֵלּוּ הֵן:

באמירת עשר מכות ישפוך עשר שפיכות מהכום עצמו כנ"ל (ויכוין בשפיכה גם כן כנ"ל) ומה שנשאר בכום (נעשה סוד יין המשמח לכך) לא ישפוך אלא יוסיף יין:

Spill from the cup while saying each of the ten plagues. (Here, too, have in mind what was mentioned above).

דָּם, צְפַרְדֵּעַ, כִּנִּים, עָרוֹב, דֶּבֶר, שְׁחִין, בָּרָד, אַרְבֶּה, חֹשֶׁךְ, מַכַּת בְּכוֹרוֹת:

רַבִּי יְהוּדָה הָיָה נוֹתֵן בָּהֶם סִמָּנִים:

Spill from the cup while saying each of the three acronyms:

דְּצַ"ךְ, עֲדַ"שׁ, בְּאַחַ"ב:

Add wine to refill the cup. (The spilled wine is discarded.)

רַבִּי יוֹסֵי הַגְּלִילִי אוֹמֵר: מִנַּיִן אַתָּה אוֹמֵר שֶׁלָּקוּ הַמִּצְרִים בְּמִצְרַיִם עֶשֶׂר מַכּוֹת וְעַל הַיָּם לָקוּ חֲמִשִּׁים מַכּוֹת, בְּמִצְרַיִם מַה הוּא אוֹמֵר: וַיֹּאמְרוּ הַחַרְטֻמִּם אֶל פַּרְעֹה אֶצְבַּע אֱלֹהִים הִיא: וְעַל הַיָּם מַה הוּא אוֹמֵר: וַיַּרְא יִשְׂרָאֵל אֶת הַיָּד הַגְּדֹלָה אֲשֶׁר עָשָׂה יְיָ בְּמִצְרַיִם, וַיִּירְאוּ הָעָם אֶת יְיָ, וַיַּאֲמִינוּ בַּיְיָ וּבְמֹשֶׁה עַבְדּוֹ: כַּמָּה לָקוּ בָּאֶצְבַּע, עֶשֶׂר מַכּוֹת, אֱמוֹר מֵעַתָּה: בְּמִצְרַיִם לָקוּ עֶשֶׂר מַכּוֹת, וְעַל הַיָּם לָקוּ חֲמִשִּׁים מַכּוֹת:

רַבִּי אֱלִיעֶזֶר אוֹמֵר: מִנַּיִן שֶׁכָּל מַכָּה וּמַכָּה שֶׁהֵבִיא הַקָּדוֹשׁ בָּרוּךְ הוּא עַל הַמִּצְרִים בְּמִצְרַיִם הָיְתָה שֶׁל אַרְבַּע מַכּוֹת, שֶׁנֶּאֱמַר: יְשַׁלַּח בָּם חֲרוֹן אַפּוֹ, עֶבְרָה, וָזַעַם, וְצָרָה, מִשְׁלַחַת מַלְאֲכֵי רָעִים: עֶבְרָה אַחַת, וָזַעַם שְׁתַּיִם, וְצָרָה שָׁלֹשׁ, מִשְׁלַחַת מַלְאֲכֵי

אלו These are the Ten Plagues which the Holy One, blessed be He, brought upon the Egyptians, namely as follows:

Spill from the cup while saying each of the ten plagues. (Here, too, have in mind what was mentioned above.)

דם Blood. Frogs. Lice. Wild Beasts. Pestilence. Boils. Hail. Locust. Darkness. Slaying of the Firstborn.

רבי Rabbi Yehudah referred to them by acronyms:

Spill from the cup while saying each of the three acronyms:

דצ"ך DeTzaCh (blood, frogs, lice); **ADaSh** (beasts, pestilence, boils); **BeAChaB** (hail, locust, darkness, firstborn).

Add wine to refill the cup. (The spilled wine is discarded.)

רבי Rabbi Yosai the Gallilean said: "How do you know that the Egyptians were stricken by ten plagues in Egypt, and then were struck by fifty plagues at the sea? In Egypt it says of them, 'The magicians said to Pharaoh "This is the finger of God."' At the sea it says, 'Israel saw the great hand that GOD laid against Egypt; and the people feared GOD, and they believed in GOD and in His servant Moses.' Now, how often were they smitten by 'the finger'? Ten plagues! Thus you must now say that in Egypt they were struck by ten plagues, and at the sea they were stricken by fifty plagues."

רבי Rabbi Eliezer said: "How do we know that each individual plague which the Holy One, blessed be He, brought upon the Egyptians in Egypt consisted of four plagues? For it is said: 'He sent against them His fierce anger, fury, and indignation, and trouble, a discharge of messengers of evil': 'Fury,' is one; 'indignation,' makes two; 'trouble,' makes three; 'discharge of messengers of evil,' makes four. Thus you must now say

רָעִים אַרְבַּע, אֱמוֹר מֵעַתָּה: בְּמִצְרַיִם לָקוּ אַרְבָּעִים
מַכּוֹת, וְעַל הַיָּם לָקוּ מָאתַיִם מַכּוֹת:

רַבִּי עֲקִיבָא אוֹמֵר: מִנַּיִן שֶׁכָּל מַכָּה וּמַכָּה שֶׁהֵבִיא
הַקָּדוֹשׁ בָּרוּךְ הוּא עַל הַמִּצְרִים בְּמִצְרַיִם הָיְתָה
שֶׁל חָמֵשׁ מַכּוֹת, שֶׁנֶּאֱמַר: יְשַׁלַּח בָּם חֲרוֹן אַפּוֹ, עֶבְרָה,
וָזַעַם, וְצָרָה, מִשְׁלַחַת מַלְאֲכֵי רָעִים: חֲרוֹן אַפּוֹ אַחַת,
עֶבְרָה שְׁתַּיִם, וָזַעַם שָׁלֹשׁ, וְצָרָה אַרְבַּע, מִשְׁלַחַת
מַלְאֲכֵי רָעִים חָמֵשׁ, אֱמוֹר מֵעַתָּה: בְּמִצְרַיִם לָקוּ
חֲמִשִּׁים מַכּוֹת, וְעַל הַיָּם לָקוּ חֲמִשִּׁים וּמָאתַיִם מַכּוֹת:

כַּמָּה מַעֲלוֹת טוֹבוֹת לַמָּקוֹם עָלֵינוּ:

The fourteen stanzas of דַּיֵּנוּ should be recited consecutively, without interruption.

אִלּוּ הוֹצִיאָנוּ מִמִּצְרַיִם
וְלֹא עָשָׂה בָהֶם שְׁפָטִים, דַּיֵּנוּ:
אִלּוּ עָשָׂה בָהֶם שְׁפָטִים
וְלֹא עָשָׂה בֵאלֹהֵיהֶם, דַּיֵּנוּ:
אִלּוּ עָשָׂה בֵאלֹהֵיהֶם
וְלֹא הָרַג אֶת בְּכוֹרֵיהֶם, דַּיֵּנוּ:
אִלּוּ הָרַג אֶת בְּכוֹרֵיהֶם
וְלֹא נָתַן לָנוּ אֶת מָמוֹנָם, דַּיֵּנוּ:
אִלּוּ נָתַן לָנוּ אֶת מָמוֹנָם
וְלֹא קָרַע לָנוּ אֶת הַיָּם, דַּיֵּנוּ:
אִלּוּ קָרַע לָנוּ אֶת הַיָּם
וְלֹא הֶעֱבִירָנוּ בְתוֹכוֹ בֶּחָרָבָה, דַּיֵּנוּ:
אִלּוּ הֶעֱבִירָנוּ בְתוֹכוֹ בֶּחָרָבָה
וְלֹא שִׁקַּע צָרֵינוּ בְּתוֹכוֹ, דַּיֵּנוּ:

מגיד

56

that in Egypt they were struck by forty plagues, and at the sea they were stricken by two hundred plagues."

רבי Rabbi Akiva said: "How do we know that each individual plague which the Holy One, blessed be He, brought upon the Egyptians in Egypt consisted of five plagues? For it is said: 'He sent against them His fierce anger, fury, and indignation, and trouble, a discharge of messengers of evil': 'His fierce anger,' is one; 'fury,' makes two; 'indignation,' makes three; 'trouble,' makes four; 'discharge of messengers of evil,' makes five. Thus you must now say that in Egypt they were struck by fifty plagues, and at the sea they were stricken by two hundred and fifty plagues."

כמה [Note] how many levels of favors the Omnipresent One has bestowed upon us!

The fourteen stanzas of *Dayenu* should be recited consecutively, without interruption. Transliteration, page 109.

אלו If He had brought us out from Egypt, and had not carried out judgments against them
—*Dayenu*, it would have sufficed us!
If He had carried out judgments against them, and not against their idols
—*Dayenu*, it would have sufficed us!
If He had destroyed their idols, and had not smitten their first-born —*Dayenu*, it would have sufficed us!
If He had smitten their first-born, and had not given us their wealth —*Dayenu*, it would have sufficed us!
If He had given us their wealth, and had not split the sea for us —*Dayenu*, it would have sufficed us!
If He had split the sea for us, and had not taken us through it on dry land
—*Dayenu*, it would have sufficed us!
If He had taken us through the sea on dry land, and had not drowned our oppressors in it
—*Dayenu*, it would have sufficed us!

אִלּוּ שִׁקַּע צָרֵינוּ בְּתוֹכוֹ

וְלֹא סִפֵּק צָרְכֵּנוּ בַּמִּדְבָּר אַרְבָּעִים שָׁנָה,   דַּיֵּנוּ:

אִלּוּ סִפֵּק צָרְכֵּנוּ בַּמִּדְבָּר אַרְבָּעִים שָׁנָה

וְלֹא הֶאֱכִילָנוּ אֶת הַמָּן,   דַּיֵּנוּ:

אִלּוּ הֶאֱכִילָנוּ אֶת הַמָּן

וְלֹא נָתַן לָנוּ אֶת הַשַּׁבָּת,   דַּיֵּנוּ:

אִלּוּ נָתַן לָנוּ אֶת הַשַּׁבָּת

וְלֹא קֵרְבָנוּ לִפְנֵי הַר סִינַי,   דַּיֵּנוּ:

אִלּוּ קֵרְבָנוּ לִפְנֵי הַר סִינַי

וְלֹא נָתַן לָנוּ אֶת הַתּוֹרָה,   דַּיֵּנוּ:

אִלּוּ נָתַן לָנוּ אֶת הַתּוֹרָה

וְלֹא הִכְנִיסָנוּ לְאֶרֶץ יִשְׂרָאֵל,   דַּיֵּנוּ:

אִלּוּ הִכְנִיסָנוּ לְאֶרֶץ יִשְׂרָאֵל

וְלֹא בָנָה לָנוּ אֶת בֵּית הַבְּחִירָה,   דַּיֵּנוּ:

עַל אַחַת כַּמָּה וְכַמָּה טוֹבָה כְפוּלָה וּמְכֻפֶּלֶת לַמָּקוֹם עָלֵינוּ, שֶׁהוֹצִיאָנוּ מִמִּצְרַיִם, וְעָשָׂה בָהֶם שְׁפָטִים, וְעָשָׂה בֵאלֹהֵיהֶם, וְהָרַג אֶת בְּכוֹרֵיהֶם, וְנָתַן לָנוּ אֶת מָמוֹנָם, וְקָרַע לָנוּ אֶת הַיָּם, וְהֶעֱבִירָנוּ בְתוֹכוֹ בֶּחָרָבָה, וְשִׁקַּע צָרֵינוּ בְּתוֹכוֹ, וְסִפֵּק צָרְכֵּנוּ בַּמִּדְבָּר אַרְבָּעִים שָׁנָה, וְהֶאֱכִילָנוּ אֶת הַמָּן, וְנָתַן לָנוּ אֶת הַשַּׁבָּת, וְקֵרְבָנוּ לִפְנֵי הַר סִינַי, וְנָתַן לָנוּ אֶת הַתּוֹרָה, וְהִכְנִיסָנוּ לְאֶרֶץ יִשְׂרָאֵל, וּבָנָה לָנוּ אֶת בֵּית הַבְּחִירָה לְכַפֵּר עַל כָּל עֲוֹנוֹתֵינוּ:

מַגִּיד

If He had drowned our oppressors in it, and had not supplied our needs in the desert for forty years

—*Dayenu*, it would have sufficed us!

If He had supplied our needs in the desert for forty years, and had not fed us the manna

—*Dayenu*, it would have sufficed us!

If He had fed us the manna, and had not given us the Shabbat

—*Dayenu*, it would have sufficed us!

If He had given us the Shabbat, and had not brought us before Mount Sinai

—*Dayenu*, it would have sufficed us!

If He had brought us before Mount Sinai, and had not given us the Torah

—*Dayenu*, it would have sufficed us!

If He had given us the Torah, and had not brought us into the land of Israel

—*Dayenu*, it would have sufficed us!

If He had brought us into the land of Israel, and had not built for us the *Beit Habechirah* (Chosen House; the *Beit Hamikdash*)

—*Dayenu*, it would have sufficed us!

על Thus how much more so should we be grateful to the Omnipresent One for the doubled and redoubled goodness that He has bestowed upon us; for He has brought us out of Egypt, and carried out judgments against them, and against their idols, and smote their first-born, and gave us their wealth, and split the sea for us, and took us through it on dry land, and drowned our oppressors in it, and supplied our needs in the desert for forty years, and fed us the manna, and gave us the Shabbat, and brought us before Mount Sinai, and gave us the Torah, and brought us into the land of Israel and built for us the *Beit Habechirah* to atone for all our sins.

רַבָּן גַּמְלִיאֵל הָיָה אוֹמֵר: כָּל שֶׁלֹּא אָמַר
שְׁלֹשָׁה דְבָרִים אֵלּוּ בַּפֶּסַח לֹא יָצָא יְדֵי
חוֹבָתוֹ. וְאֵלּוּ הֵן:

פֶּסַח, מַצָּה וּמָרוֹר:

פֶּסַח שֶׁהָיוּ אֲבוֹתֵינוּ אוֹכְלִים בִּזְמַן שֶׁבֵּית הַמִּקְדָּשׁ
קַיָּם עַל שׁוּם מָה, עַל שׁוּם שֶׁפָּסַח הַמָּקוֹם
עַל בָּתֵּי אֲבוֹתֵינוּ בְּמִצְרַיִם, שֶׁנֶּאֱמַר: וַאֲמַרְתֶּם זֶבַח
פֶּסַח הוּא לַיָי אֲשֶׁר פָּסַח עַל בָּתֵּי בְנֵי יִשְׂרָאֵל
בְּמִצְרַיִם בְּנָגְפּוֹ אֶת מִצְרַיִם וְאֶת בָּתֵּינוּ הִצִּיל, וַיִּקֹּד
הָעָם וַיִּשְׁתַּחֲווּ:

נוֹטֵל הַפְּרוּסָה בְּיָדוֹ וְיֹאמַר:

Hold the second and third matzot—by means of the cloth over them—while reciting the
beginning of the following paragraph (until after the word marked with the asterisk).

מַצָּה זוֹ שֶׁאָנוּ אוֹכְלִים עַל שׁוּם מָה, עַל שׁוּם* שֶׁלֹּא
הִסְפִּיק בְּצֵקֶת שֶׁל אֲבוֹתֵינוּ לְהַחֲמִיץ עַד
שֶׁנִּגְלָה עֲלֵיהֶם מֶלֶךְ מַלְכֵי הַמְּלָכִים הַקָּדוֹשׁ בָּרוּךְ
הוּא וּגְאָלָם, שֶׁנֶּאֱמַר: וַיֹּאפוּ אֶת הַבָּצֵק אֲשֶׁר הוֹצִיאוּ
מִמִּצְרַיִם עֻגֹת מַצּוֹת, כִּי לֹא חָמֵץ, כִּי גֹרְשׁוּ מִמִּצְרַיִם
וְלֹא יָכְלוּ לְהִתְמַהְמֵהַּ, וְגַם צֵדָה לֹא עָשׂוּ לָהֶם:

נוֹטֵל הַמָּרוֹר בְּיָדוֹ וְיֹאמַר:

Place your hands on the maror and chazeret while reciting the beginning of the
following paragraph (until after the word marked with the asterisk).

מָרוֹר זֶה שֶׁאָנוּ אוֹכְלִים עַל שׁוּם מָה, עַל שׁוּם*
שֶׁמֵּרְרוּ הַמִּצְרִים אֶת חַיֵּי אֲבוֹתֵינוּ בְּמִצְרַיִם,
שֶׁנֶּאֱמַר: וַיְמָרְרוּ אֶת חַיֵּיהֶם בַּעֲבֹדָה קָשָׁה בְּחֹמֶר
וּבִלְבֵנִים וּבְכָל עֲבֹדָה בַּשָּׂדֶה, אֵת כָּל עֲבֹדָתָם אֲשֶׁר
עָבְדוּ בָהֶם בְּפָרֶךְ:

מַגִּיד

60

רבן Rabban Gamliel used to say: "Whoever does not discuss the following three things on Pesach has not fulfilled his duty, namely:

Pesach (the Pesach-sacrifice);
Matzah (the unleavened bread);
Maror (the bitter herbs)."

פסח **Pesach**—the Pesach-lamb that our fathers ate during the time of the Beit Hamikdash—for what reason [did they do so]? Because the Omnipresent passed over our fathers' houses in Egypt, as it is said: "You shall say, 'It is a Pesach-offering to GOD, because He passed over the houses of the children of Israel in Egypt when He struck the Egyptians with a plague, and He saved our houses.' And the people bowed and prostrated themselves."

Hold the second and third matzot—by means of the cloth over them—while reciting the beginning of the following paragraph (until after the word marked with the asterisk).

מצה This **matzah** that we eat—for what reason? Because* the dough of our fathers did not have time to become leavened before the King of the kings of kings, the Holy One, blessed be He, revealed Himself to them and redeemed them. Thus it is said: "They baked matzah-cakes from the dough that they had brought out of Egypt, because it was not leavened; for they had been driven out of Egypt and could not delay, and they had also not prepared any [other] provisions."

Place your hands on the maror and chazeret while reciting the beginning of the following paragraph (until after the word marked with the asterisk).

מרור This **maror** that we eat—for what reason? Because* the Egyptians embittered our fathers' lives in Egypt, as it is said: "They made their lives bitter with hard work, with mortar and with bricks, and with all manner of service in the field; all their work which they made them perform with rigor."

בְּכָל דּוֹר וָדוֹר חַיָּב אָדָם לִרְאוֹת אֶת עַצְמוֹ כְּאִלּוּ
הוּא יָצָא מִמִּצְרַיִם, שֶׁנֶּאֱמַר: וְהִגַּדְתָּ לְבִנְךָ
בַּיּוֹם הַהוּא לֵאמֹר בַּעֲבוּר זֶה עָשָׂה יְיָ לִי בְּצֵאתִי
מִמִּצְרָיִם: לֹא אֶת אֲבוֹתֵינוּ בִּלְבָד גָּאַל הַקָּדוֹשׁ בָּרוּךְ
הוּא מִמִּצְרַיִם, אֶלָּא אַף אוֹתָנוּ גָּאַל עִמָּהֶם,
שֶׁנֶּאֱמַר: וְאוֹתָנוּ הוֹצִיא מִשָּׁם לְמַעַן הָבִיא אוֹתָנוּ
לָתֶת לָנוּ אֶת הָאָרֶץ אֲשֶׁר נִשְׁבַּע לַאֲבוֹתֵינוּ:

יכסה את הפת ויגביה את הכוס ואוחזו בידו עד סיום ברכת אשר גאלנו:
Cover the matzot.
Hold the cup in the palm of the right hand for the following paragraph:

לְפִיכָךְ אֲנַחְנוּ חַיָּבִים: לְהוֹדוֹת לְהַלֵּל לְשַׁבֵּחַ לְפָאֵר
לְרוֹמֵם לְהַדֵּר לְבָרֵךְ לְעַלֵּה וּלְקַלֵּס, לְמִי
שֶׁעָשָׂה לַאֲבוֹתֵינוּ וְלָנוּ אֶת כָּל הַנִּסִּים הָאֵלּוּ.
הוֹצִיאָנוּ מֵעַבְדוּת לְחֵרוּת, מִיָּגוֹן לְשִׂמְחָה, וּמֵאֵבֶל
לְיוֹם טוֹב, וּמֵאֲפֵלָה לְאוֹר גָּדוֹל, וּמִשִּׁעְבּוּד לִגְאֻלָּה,
וְנֹאמַר לְפָנָיו הַלְלוּיָהּ:

Place the cup on the table.

הַלְלוּיָהּ, הַלְלוּ עַבְדֵי יְיָ, הַלְלוּ אֶת שֵׁם יְיָ: יְהִי
שֵׁם יְיָ מְבֹרָךְ, מֵעַתָּה וְעַד עוֹלָם:
מִמִּזְרַח שֶׁמֶשׁ עַד מְבוֹאוֹ, מְהֻלָּל שֵׁם יְיָ: רָם עַל
כָּל גּוֹיִם יְיָ, עַל הַשָּׁמַיִם כְּבוֹדוֹ: מִי כַּיְיָ אֱלֹהֵינוּ,
הַמַּגְבִּיהִי לָשָׁבֶת: הַמַּשְׁפִּילִי לִרְאוֹת, בַּשָּׁמַיִם
וּבָאָרֶץ: מְקִימִי מֵעָפָר דָּל, מֵאַשְׁפֹּת יָרִים אֶבְיוֹן:
לְהוֹשִׁיבִי עִם נְדִיבִים, עִם נְדִיבֵי עַמּוֹ: מוֹשִׁיבִי
עֲקֶרֶת הַבַּיִת, אֵם הַבָּנִים שְׂמֵחָה, הַלְלוּיָהּ:

מגיד

בכל In every generation a person is obligated to regard himself as if he had come out of Egypt, as it is said: "You shall tell your child on that day, 'It is because of this that GOD acted for me when I left Egypt.'" The Holy One, blessed be He, redeemed not only our fathers from Egypt, but He redeemed also us with them, as it is said: "It was us that He brought out from there, so that He might bring us to give us the land that He swore to our fathers."

Cover the matzot.
Hold the cup in the palm of the right hand for the following paragraph:

לפיכך Thus it is our duty to thank, to laud, to praise, to glorify, to exalt, to adore, to bless, to elevate and to honor the One who did all these miracles for our fathers and for us. He took us from slavery to freedom, from sorrow to joy, from mourning to festivity, from deep darkness to great light and from bondage to redemption. Let us therefore recite before Him: Halleluyah—Praise God!

Place the cup on the table.

הללויה Halleluyah—Praise God! Offer praise, you servants of GOD; praise the name of GOD. May GOD's name be blessed from now and to all eternity. From the rising of the sun to its setting, GOD's Name is praised. GOD is high above all nations; His glory is over the heavens. Who is like GOD, our God, who dwells on high yet looks down so low upon heaven and earth! He raises the poor from the dust, He lifts the needy from the dunghill, to seat them with nobles, with the nobles of His people. He restores the barren woman to the house, into a joyful mother of children. Halleluyah—praise God!

בְּצֵאת יִשְׂרָאֵל מִמִּצְרָיִם, בֵּית יַעֲקֹב מֵעַם לֹעֵז:
הָיְתָה יְהוּדָה לְקָדְשׁוֹ, יִשְׂרָאֵל מַמְשְׁלוֹתָיו:
הַיָּם רָאָה וַיָּנֹס, הַיַּרְדֵּן יִסֹּב לְאָחוֹר: הֶהָרִים רָקְדוּ
כְאֵילִים, גְּבָעוֹת כִּבְנֵי צֹאן: מַה לְּךָ הַיָּם כִּי תָנוּס,
הַיַּרְדֵּן תִּסֹּב לְאָחוֹר: הֶהָרִים תִּרְקְדוּ כְאֵילִים, גְּבָעוֹת
כִּבְנֵי צֹאן: מִלִּפְנֵי אָדוֹן חוּלִי אָרֶץ, מִלִּפְנֵי אֱלוֹהַּ
יַעֲקֹב: הַהֹפְכִי הַצּוּר אֲגַם מָיִם, חַלָּמִישׁ לְמַעְיְנוֹ מָיִם:

Hold the cup in the palm of the right hand for the following two blessings.

בָּרוּךְ אַתָּה יְיָ, אֱלֹהֵינוּ מֶלֶךְ הָעוֹלָם, אֲשֶׁר גְּאָלָנוּ
וְגָאַל אֶת אֲבוֹתֵינוּ מִמִּצְרַיִם, וְהִגִּיעָנוּ
הַלַּיְלָה הַזֶּה לֶאֱכָל בּוֹ מַצָּה וּמָרוֹר, כֵּן יְיָ אֱלֹהֵינוּ
וֵאלֹהֵי אֲבוֹתֵינוּ יַגִּיעֵנוּ לְמוֹעֲדִים וְלִרְגָלִים אֲחֵרִים
הַבָּאִים לִקְרָאתֵנוּ לְשָׁלוֹם, שְׂמֵחִים בְּבִנְיַן עִירֶךָ,
וְשָׂשִׂים בַּעֲבוֹדָתֶךָ, וְנֹאכַל שָׁם

On Saturday night: | On all nights except Saturday night:
מִן הַזְּבָחִים וּמִן הַפְּסָחִים | מִן הַפְּסָחִים וּמִן הַזְּבָחִים

אֲשֶׁר יַגִּיעַ דָּמָם עַל קִיר מִזְבַּחֲךָ לְרָצוֹן, וְנוֹדֶה לְךָ
שִׁיר חָדָשׁ עַל גְּאֻלָּתֵנוּ וְעַל פְּדוּת נַפְשֵׁנוּ. בָּרוּךְ
אַתָּה יְיָ, גָּאַל יִשְׂרָאֵל:

ומברך ושותה בהסיבה:

בָּרוּךְ אַתָּה יְיָ, אֱלֹהֵינוּ מֶלֶךְ הָעוֹלָם, בּוֹרֵא פְּרִי
הַגָּפֶן:

Drink the entire cup without pause while seated, reclining on the left side. (One who cannot drink the entire cup should drink at least most of it.)

Review the five steps of רָחְצָה through כּוֹרֵךְ at this point, to avoid making an interruption between them.

מגיד

64

בצאת When Israel went out of Egypt, the House of Jacob from a people of a foreign language, Judah became His holy one, Israel His dominion. The sea saw and fled, the Jordan turned backward. The mountains skipped like rams, the hills like young sheep. What is with you, O sea, that you flee; Jordan, that you turn backward? Mountains, why do you skip like rams; hills, like young sheep? [We do so] before the Master, the Creator of the earth, before the God of Jacob, who turns the rock into a pool of water, the flint-stone into a spring of water.

Hold the cup in the palm of the right hand for the following two blessings.

ברוך Blessed are You, GOD, our God, King of the universe, who has redeemed us and redeemed our fathers from Egypt, and enabled us to attain this night to eat matzah and maror. So too, GOD, our God and God of our fathers, enable us to attain other holidays and festivals that will come to us in peace—with happiness in the rebuilding of Your city, and with rejoicing in Your service [in the *Beit Hamikdash*]. Then we shall eat

On all nights except Saturday night:	On Saturday night:
of the sacrifices and of the Pesach-offerings	of the Pesach-offerings and of the sacrifices

whose blood shall be sprinkled on the wall of Your altar for acceptance; and we shall thank You with a new song for our redemption and for the deliverance of our souls. Blessed are You, GOD, who redeemed Israel.

ברוך Blessed are You, GOD, our God, King of the universe, who creates the fruit of the vine.

Maggid

Drink the entire cup without pause while seated, reclining on the left side. (One who cannot drink the entire cup should drink at least most of it.)

Review the five steps of Rachtzah through Korech at this point, to avoid making an interruption between them.

רחצה

רחצה ואחר כך נוטל ידיו ומברך על נטילת ידים:

The hands are now washed in the following manner:

Pick up the cup containing the water in the right hand. Pass it to the left hand, and pour three times on the right hand. Then pass the cup to the right hand and pour three times on the left hand. It is customary to hold the cup with a towel when pouring on the left hand.

A little water from the final pouring should remain in the left hand. It should be rubbed over both hands together, while reciting the following blessing:

בָּרוּךְ אַתָּה יְיָ, אֱלֹהֵינוּ מֶלֶךְ הָעוֹלָם, אֲשֶׁר קִדְּשָׁנוּ בְּמִצְוֹתָיו, וְצִוָּנוּ עַל נְטִילַת יָדָיִם:

Dry the hands. Do not talk from this point until after eating the matzah.

מוציא

מוציא ויקח המצות כסדר שהניחם הפרוסה בין שתי השלימות ויאחזם בידו ויברך:

Hold the three matzot (while still covered by the cloth) and recite the following blessing:

בָּרוּךְ אַתָּה יְיָ, אֱלֹהֵינוּ מֶלֶךְ הָעוֹלָם, הַמּוֹצִיא לֶחֶם מִן הָאָרֶץ:

Do not break the matzot.

מצה

מצה ולא יבצע מהן אלא יניח המצה השלישית להשמט מידו ויברך על הפרוסה עם העליונה טרם ישברם ברכה זו. ויכוין לפטור ג"כ אכילת הכריכה שממצה השלישית וגם אכילת האפיקומן יפטור בברכה זו:

Put down the bottom matzah and recite the following blessing over the top two matzot. When reciting the blessing, have in mind that it is also for the eating of the "sandwich" of Korech—which will be made with the third (bottom) matzah—and also for the eating of the afikoman at the end of the meal.

בָּרוּךְ אַתָּה יְיָ, אֱלֹהֵינוּ מֶלֶךְ הָעוֹלָם, אֲשֶׁר קִדְּשָׁנוּ בְּמִצְוֹתָיו, וְצִוָּנוּ עַל אֲכִילַת מַצָּה:

ואח"כ יבצע כזית מכל אחד אחד משתיהן, ויאכלם ביחד ובהסיבה:

Break off a *kezayit* from each of the two matzot held, and eat the two pieces together while reclining on the left side. The entire amount (i.e., two *kezeitim*) should be eaten within approximately four to seven minutes.

The hands are now washed in the following manner:

Pick up the cup containing the water in the right hand. Pass it to the left hand, and pour three times on the right hand. Then pass the cup to the right hand and pour three times on the left hand. It is customary to hold the cup with a towel when pouring on the left hand.

A little water from the final pouring should remain in the left hand. It should be rubbed over both hands together, while reciting the following blessing:

Transliteration, page 109.

ברוך Blessed are You, GOD, our God, King of the universe, who has sanctified us with His commandments, and commanded us concerning the washing of the hands.

Dry the hands. Do not talk from this point until after eating the matzah.

Hold the three matzot (while still covered by the cloth) and recite the following blessing:

Transliteration, page 109.

ברוך Blessed are You, GOD, our God, King of the universe, who brings forth bread from the earth.

Do not break the matzot.

Put down the bottom matzah and recite the following blessing over the top two matzot. When reciting the blessing, have in mind that it is also for the eating of the "sandwich" of Korech—which will be made with the third (bottom) matzah—and also for the eating of the afikoman at the end of the meal.

Transliteration, page 109.

ברוך Blessed are You, GOD, our God, King of the universe, who has sanctified us with His commandments, and commanded us concerning the eating of matzah.

Break off a *kezayit* from each of the two matzot held, and eat the two pieces together while reclining on the left side. The entire amount (i.e., two *kezeitim*) should be eaten within approximately four to seven minutes.

Each participant is required to eat a *kezayit* of matzah. Since it is impossible for all to receive the sufficient amount from the two matzot of the Seder plate, other matzot should be available. However, it is preferable that all receive at least a small piece of the original two matzot.

The matzah is not dipped in salt.

מרור

מָרוֹר ואחר כך יקח כזית מרור ויטבל בחרוסת וינער החרוסת מעליו כדי שלא יתבטל טעם המרירות ויברך ברכה זו:

Take the *kezayit* of maror and dip it into the charoset—which should be softened with wine before dipping—then shake off the charoset so that the bitter taste of the maror will not be neutralized. When reciting the following blessing, have in mind that it is also for the chazeret of the "sandwich" of Korech.

בָּרוּךְ אַתָּה יְיָ, אֱלֹהֵינוּ מֶלֶךְ הָעוֹלָם, אֲשֶׁר קִדְּשָׁנוּ בְּמִצְוֹתָיו, וְצִוָּנוּ עַל אֲכִילַת מָרוֹר:

ויאכלנו בלי הסיבה:

Eat the maror without reclining. The entire *kezayit* should be eaten within approximately four to seven minutes.

Each participant is required to eat a *kezayit* of maror. Since it is impossible for all to receive the sufficient amount from the maror on the Seder plate, other maror should be available.

כורך

כּוֹרֵךְ ואח"כ יקח מצה הג' וחזרת עמה כשיעור כזית ויטבול בחרוסת ויכרכם ביחד ויאמר זה:

Take a *kezayit* of the third matzah and a *kezayit* of the chazeret. Place some dry charoset on the chazeret and then shake it off. Combine the two—like a sandwich—and recite the following:

זֵכֶר עָשָׂה הַלֵּל בִּזְמַן שֶׁבֵּית הַמִּקְדָּשׁ הָיָה קַיָּם, הָיָה כּוֹרֵךְ פֶּסַח מַצָּה וּמָרוֹר וְאוֹכֵל בְּיַחַד, כְּמוֹ שֶׁנֶּאֱמַר: עַל מַצּוֹת וּמְרוֹרִים יֹאכְלֻהוּ:

ויאכלם ביחד [ובהסיבה. טוש"ע סימן תע"ה. הגהה מסדור אדמו"ר בעל צ"צ ז"ל]:

Eat the korech "sandwich" while reclining on the left side. The korech should be eaten within approximately four to seven minutes.

Each participant is required to eat a *kezayit* of matzah and a *kezayit* of chazeret. Since it is impossible for all to receive the sufficient amount from the matzah and chazeret of the Seder plate, other matzot and chazeret should be available.

Each participant is required to eat a *kezayit* of matzah. Since it is impossible for all to receive the sufficient amount from the two matzot of the Seder plate, other matzot should be available. However, it is preferable that all receive at least a small piece of the original two matzot.

The matzah is not dipped in salt.

Maror

Take the *kezayit* of maror and dip it into the charoset—which should be softened with wine before dipping—then shake off the charoset so that the bitter taste of the maror will not be neutralized. When reciting the following blessing, have in mind that it is also for the chazeret of the "sandwich" of Korech.

Transliteration, page 110.

ברוך Blessed are You, GOD, our God, King of the universe, who has sanctified us with His commandments, and commanded us concerning the eating of maror.

Eat the maror without reclining. The entire *kezayit* should be eaten within approximately four to seven minutes.

Each participant is required to eat a *kezayit* of maror. Since it is impossible for all to receive the sufficient amount from the maror on the Seder plate, other maror should be available.

Korech

Take a *kezayit* of the third matzah and a *kezayit* of the chazeret. Place some dry charoset on the chazeret and then shake it off. Combine the two like a sandwich, and recite the following:

Transliteration, page 110.

כן Thus did Hillel do at the time of the Beit Hamikdash: he would combine the Pesach-offering, matzah and maror and eat them together, as it is said: "They shall eat it with matzot and bitter herbs."

Eat the korech "sandwich" while reclining on the left side. The korech should be eaten within approximately four to seven minutes.

Each participant is required to eat a *kezayit* of matzah and a *kezayit* of chazeret. Since it is impossible for all to receive the sufficient amount from the matzah and chazeret of the Seder plate, other matzot and chazeret should be available.

שלחן עורך

שלחן עורך ואחר כך אוכל ושותה כדי צרכו ויכול לשתות יין בין כוס ב' לג':

It is customary not to recline while eating the meal.

The meal is started by eating the egg from the Seder plate, dipped in salt water.

It is the Chabad custom to be careful that the matzah not become wet during the first seven days of Pesach. The matzot on the table, therefore, should be kept covered, lest some water drip on them.

From the morning of Erev Pesach until after the korech of the second Seder, one does not eat any of the ingredients of the charoset and maror.

Eat enough so that the afikoman will be eaten when already satiated—for it commemorates the Pesach-offering, which was to be eaten when satiated. However, do not overeat, so that the eating of the afikoman will not be gluttony.

It is permitted to drink wine during the meal.

One should drink enough during the meal so that one will not be thirsty after eating the afikoman (see next section).

צפון

צפון ואח"כ יקח האפיקומן ויחלקו לכל בני ביתו לכל אחד כזית ויזהר שלא ישתה אחר אפיקומן ויאכל בהסיבה וצריך לאכלו קודם חצות:

Each participant receives a piece of the afikoman.

Ideally, one should eat two *kezeitim* of the afikoman—one *kezayit* to commemorate the Pesach-offering, and the other *kezayit* to commemorate the matzah which was to be eaten with the Pesach-offering. One who finds this too difficult, however, may eat the amount of one *kezayit*, bearing in mind that this *kezayit* serves as a remembrance for the opinion that is ultimately correct as to what the afikoman commemorates (i.e., the Pesach-offering, or the matzah eaten with it).

Since it is impossible for all to receive the sufficient amount from the matzah put away for the afikoman, other matzot should be available.

One should not eat or drink after eating the afikoman. The Chabad custom is to avoid drinking even water.

On the first night of Pesach, the afikoman should be eaten before midnight.

Eat the afikoman while reclining on the left side. The afikoman should be eaten within approximately four to seven minutes.

ברך

ברך ואח"כ מוזגין כוס שלישי ואומר עליו בהמ"ז:

The third cup is poured, and the Blessing After Meals is recited.

An additional cup, the "cup of Elijah," is also filled.

Shulchan Orech

It is customary not to recline while eating the meal.

The meal is started by eating the egg from the Seder plate, dipped in salt water.

It is the Chabad custom to be careful that the matzah not become wet during the first seven days of Pesach. The matzot on the table, therefore, should be kept covered, lest some water drip on them.

From the morning of Erev Pesach until after the korech of the second Seder, one does not eat any of the ingredients of the charoset and maror.

Eat enough so that the afikoman will be eaten when already satiated—for it commemorates the Pesach-offering, which was to be eaten when satiated. However, do not overeat, so that the eating of the afikoman will not be gluttony.

It is permitted to drink wine during the meal.

One should drink enough during the meal so that one will not be thirsty after eating the afikoman (see next section).

Czafun

Each participant receives a piece of the afikoman.

Ideally, one should eat two *kezeitim* of the afikoman—one *kezayit* to commemorate the Pesach-offering, and the other *kezayit* to commemorate the matzah which was to be eaten with the Pesach-offering. One who finds this too difficult, however, may eat the amount of one *kezayit*, bearing in mind that this *kezayit* serves as a remembrance for the opinion that is ultimately correct as to what the afikoman commemorates (i.e., the Pesach-offering, or the matzah eaten with it).

Since it is impossible for all to receive the sufficient amount from the matzah put away for the afikoman, other matzot should be available.

One should not eat or drink after eating the afikoman. The Chabad custom is to avoid drinking even water.

On the first night of Pesach, the afikoman should be eaten before midnight.

Eat the afikoman while reclining on the left side. The afikoman should be eaten within approximately four to seven minutes.

Berach

The third cup is poured, and the Blessing After Meals is recited.
An additional cup, the "cup of Elijah," is also filled.

שִׁיר הַמַּעֲלוֹת, בְּשׁוּב יְיָ אֶת שִׁיבַת צִיּוֹן, הָיִינוּ כְּחֹלְמִים: אָז יִמָּלֵא שְׂחוֹק פִּינוּ וּלְשׁוֹנֵנוּ רִנָּה, אָז יֹאמְרוּ בַגּוֹיִם, הִגְדִּיל יְיָ לַעֲשׂוֹת עִם אֵלֶּה: הִגְדִּיל יְיָ לַעֲשׂוֹת עִמָּנוּ, הָיִינוּ שְׂמֵחִים: שׁוּבָה יְיָ אֶת שְׁבִיתֵנוּ, כַּאֲפִיקִים בַּנֶּגֶב: הַזֹּרְעִים בְּדִמְעָה, בְּרִנָּה יִקְצֹרוּ: הָלוֹךְ יֵלֵךְ וּבָכֹה נֹשֵׂא מֶשֶׁךְ הַזָּרַע, בֹּא יָבֹא בְרִנָּה נֹשֵׂא אֲלֻמֹּתָיו:

לִבְנֵי קֹרַח מִזְמוֹר שִׁיר, יְסוּדָתוֹ בְּהַרְרֵי קֹדֶשׁ: אֹהֵב יְיָ שַׁעֲרֵי צִיּוֹן, מִכֹּל מִשְׁכְּנוֹת יַעֲקֹב: נִכְבָּדוֹת מְדֻבָּר בָּךְ, עִיר הָאֱלֹהִים סֶלָה: אַזְכִּיר רַהַב וּבָבֶל לְיֹדְעָי, הִנֵּה פְלֶשֶׁת וְצֹר עִם כּוּשׁ, זֶה יֻלַּד שָׁם: וּלְצִיּוֹן יֵאָמַר אִישׁ וְאִישׁ יֻלַּד בָּהּ, וְהוּא יְכוֹנְנֶהָ עֶלְיוֹן: יְיָ יִסְפֹּר בִּכְתוֹב עַמִּים, זֶה יֻלַּד שָׁם סֶלָה: וְשָׁרִים כְּחֹלְלִים, כָּל מַעְיָנַי בָּךְ:

אֲבָרְכָה אֶת יְיָ בְּכָל עֵת, תָּמִיד תְּהִלָּתוֹ בְּפִי: סוֹף דָּבָר הַכֹּל נִשְׁמָע, אֶת הָאֱלֹהִים יְרָא וְאֶת מִצְוֹתָיו שְׁמוֹר כִּי זֶה כָּל הָאָדָם: תְּהִלַּת יְיָ יְדַבֶּר פִּי וִיבָרֵךְ כָּל בָּשָׂר שֵׁם קָדְשׁוֹ לְעוֹלָם וָעֶד: וַאֲנַחְנוּ נְבָרֵךְ יָהּ מֵעַתָּה וְעַד עוֹלָם הַלְלוּיָהּ:

זֶה חֵלֶק אָדָם רָשָׁע מֵאֱלֹהִים וְנַחֲלַת אִמְרוֹ מֵאֵל:

Rinse the fingertips (but do not pass them over the lips as during the rest of the year), then recite the following:

וַיְדַבֵּר אֵלַי זֶה הַשֻּׁלְחָן אֲשֶׁר לִפְנֵי יְיָ:

The cup is held in the palm of the right hand until after the blessing וּבְנֵה, page 78.

ZIMMUN—INVITATION

When three or more men eat together, one of them leads the rest in the blessing. When ten or more eat together, add אֱלֹהֵינוּ as indicated. If there are less then three men at the Seder, continue with בָּרוּךְ, next page

שיר A Song of Ascents. When GOD will return the exiles of Zion, we will have been like dreamers. Then our mouth will be filled with laughter, and our tongue with joyous song. Then will they say among the nations, "GOD has done great things for these." GOD has done great things for us; we were joyful. GOD, return our exiles as streams in the Negev. Those who sow in tears will reap with joyous song. He goes along weeping, carrying the bag of seed; he will surely come [back] with joyous song, carrying his sheaves.

לבני A Psalm by the sons of Korach, a song whose foundation is in the holy mountains. GOD loves the gates of Zion more than all the dwelling-places of Jacob. Glorious things are spoken of you, O city of God. I will make mention of Rahab and Babylon unto those that know me; behold Philistia and Tyre, as well as Cush, "This one was born there." But of Zion it will be said, "This man and that man was born there," and He, the Most High, will establish it. GOD will count the register of the nations, "This one was born there." Selah. Singers and dancers alike [will chant], "All my inner thoughts are of you."

אברכה I will bless GOD at all times; His praise is always in my mouth. The ultimate conclusion, all having been heard: fear God and observe His commandments, for this is the whole of man. My mouth will utter the praise of GOD, and all flesh shall bless His holy Name forever and ever. And we will bless GOD from now and forever. Halleluyah—praise God!

זה This is the portion of a wicked man from God, and the heritage assigned to him by God.

Rinse the fingertips (but do not pass them over the lips as during the rest of the year), then recite the following:

וידבר And he said to me: This is the table that is before GOD.

The cup is held in the palm of the right hand until after the blessing *Rebuild*, page 79.

ZIMMUN — INVITATION

When three or more men eat together, one of them leads the rest in the blessing. When ten or more eat together, add *our God* as indicated. If there are less then three men at the Seder, continue with *Blessed*, next page. Transliteration, page 110.

Leader:

רַבּוֹתַי מִיר וֶועלִין בֶּעֶנְטְשִׁין:

Others:

יְהִי שֵׁם יְיָ מְבֹרָךְ מֵעַתָּה וְעַד עוֹלָם:

Leader:

יְהִי שֵׁם יְיָ מְבֹרָךְ מֵעַתָּה וְעַד עוֹלָם:
בִּרְשׁוּת מָרָנָן וְרַבָּנָן וְרַבּוֹתַי נְבָרֵךְ (אֱלֹהֵינוּ) שֶׁאָכַלְנוּ מִשֶּׁלּוֹ:

Others who have eaten:

בָּרוּךְ (אֱלֹהֵינוּ) שֶׁאָכַלְנוּ מִשֶּׁלּוֹ וּבְטוּבוֹ חָיִינוּ:

Leader:

בָּרוּךְ (אֱלֹהֵינוּ) שֶׁאָכַלְנוּ מִשֶּׁלּוֹ וּבְטוּבוֹ חָיִינוּ:

The leader concludes each blessing aloud, and the others respond אָמֵן.

בָּרוּךְ אַתָּה יְיָ אֱלֹהֵינוּ מֶלֶךְ הָעוֹלָם, הַזָּן אֶת הָעוֹלָם כֻּלּוֹ בְּטוּבוֹ בְּחֵן בְּחֶסֶד וּבְרַחֲמִים הוּא נוֹתֵן לֶחֶם לְכָל בָּשָׂר כִּי לְעוֹלָם חַסְדּוֹ: וּבְטוּבוֹ הַגָּדוֹל עִמָּנוּ תָּמִיד לֹא חָסֵר לָנוּ וְאַל יֶחְסַר לָנוּ מָזוֹן לְעוֹלָם וָעֶד: בַּעֲבוּר שְׁמוֹ הַגָּדוֹל כִּי הוּא אֵל זָן וּמְפַרְנֵס לַכֹּל וּמֵטִיב לַכֹּל וּמֵכִין מָזוֹן לְכָל בְּרִיּוֹתָיו אֲשֶׁר בָּרָא, כָּאָמוּר: פּוֹתֵחַ אֶת יָדֶךָ וּמַשְׂבִּיעַ לְכָל חַי רָצוֹן: בָּרוּךְ אַתָּה יְיָ, הַזָּן אֶת הַכֹּל:

נוֹדֶה לְךָ יְיָ אֱלֹהֵינוּ עַל שֶׁהִנְחַלְתָּ לַאֲבוֹתֵינוּ אֶרֶץ חֶמְדָּה טוֹבָה וּרְחָבָה וְעַל שֶׁהוֹצֵאתָנוּ יְיָ אֱלֹהֵינוּ מֵאֶרֶץ מִצְרַיִם וּפְדִיתָנוּ מִבֵּית עֲבָדִים וְעַל בְּרִיתְךָ שֶׁחָתַמְתָּ בִּבְשָׂרֵנוּ וְעַל תּוֹרָתְךָ שֶׁלִּמַּדְתָּנוּ וְעַל חֻקֶּיךָ שֶׁהוֹדַעְתָּנוּ וְעַל חַיִּים חֵן וָחֶסֶד שֶׁחוֹנַנְתָּנוּ וְעַל אֲכִילַת מָזוֹן שֶׁאַתָּה זָן וּמְפַרְנֵס אוֹתָנוּ תָּמִיד בְּכָל יוֹם וּבְכָל עֵת וּבְכָל שָׁעָה:

Leader:

Gentlemen, let us say the Blessings.

Others:

May the Name of GOD be blessed from now and to all eternity.

Leader:

May the Name of GOD be blessed from now and to all eternity. With your permission, esteemed gentlemen, let us bless Him (our God) of whose bounty we have eaten.

Others who have eaten:

Blessed be He (our God) of whose bounty we have eaten and by whose goodness we live.

Leader:

Blessed be He (our God) of whose bounty we have eaten and by whose goodness we live.

The leader concludes each blessing aloud, and the others respond Amen.

ברוך Blessed are You, GOD, our God, King of the universe, who, in His goodness, feeds the whole world with grace, with kindness and with mercy. He gives food to all flesh, for His kindness is everlasting. Through His great goodness to us, continuously, we are not lacking, and may we never lack food, for the sake of His great Name. For He is a [benevolent] God who feeds and sustains all, does good to all, and prepares food for all His creatures whom He has created, as it is said: "You open Your hand and satisfy the desire of every living thing." Blessed are You, GOD, who provides food for all.

נודה We thank You, GOD, our God, for having given as a heritage to our fathers a precious, good and spacious land; for having brought us out, GOD our God, from the land of Egypt, and redeemed us from the house of slaves; for Your covenant which You have sealed in our flesh; for Your Torah which You have taught us; for Your statutes which You have made known to us; for the life, favor and kindness which You have graciously bestowed upon us; and for the food we eat with which You constantly feed and sustain us every day, at all times and at every hour.

וְעַל הַכֹּל יְיָ אֱלֹהֵינוּ אֲנַחְנוּ מוֹדִים לָךְ וּמְבָרְכִים
אוֹתָךְ יִתְבָּרַךְ שִׁמְךָ בְּפִי כָּל חַי תָּמִיד לְעוֹלָם
וָעֶד, כַּכָּתוּב: וְאָכַלְתָּ וְשָׂבָעְתָּ וּבֵרַכְתָּ אֶת יְיָ אֱלֹהֶיךָ
עַל הָאָרֶץ הַטֹּבָה אֲשֶׁר נָתַן לָךְ: בָּרוּךְ אַתָּה יְיָ,
עַל הָאָרֶץ וְעַל הַמָּזוֹן:

רַחֵם יְיָ אֱלֹהֵינוּ עַל יִשְׂרָאֵל עַמֶּךְ וְעַל יְרוּשָׁלַיִם
עִירֶךָ וְעַל צִיּוֹן מִשְׁכַּן כְּבוֹדֶךָ וְעַל מַלְכוּת
בֵּית דָּוִד מְשִׁיחֶךָ וְעַל הַבַּיִת הַגָּדוֹל וְהַקָּדוֹשׁ
שֶׁנִּקְרָא שִׁמְךָ עָלָיו: אֱלֹהֵינוּ אָבִינוּ רוֹעֵנוּ זוֹנֵנוּ
פַרְנְסֵנוּ וְכַלְכְּלֵנוּ וְהַרְוִיחֵנוּ וְהַרְוַח לָנוּ יְיָ אֱלֹהֵינוּ
מְהֵרָה מִכָּל צָרוֹתֵינוּ: וְנָא אַל תַּצְרִיכֵנוּ יְיָ אֱלֹהֵינוּ,
לֹא לִידֵי מַתְּנַת בָּשָׂר וָדָם וְלֹא לִידֵי הַלְוָאָתָם כִּי
אִם לְיָדְךָ הַמְּלֵאָה הַפְּתוּחָה הַקְּדוֹשָׁה וְהָרְחָבָה
שֶׁלֹּא נֵבוֹשׁ וְלֹא נִכָּלֵם לְעוֹלָם וָעֶד:

On Friday night:

רְצֵה וְהַחֲלִיצֵנוּ יְיָ אֱלֹהֵינוּ בְּמִצְוֹתֶיךָ וּבְמִצְוַת יוֹם
הַשְּׁבִיעִי הַשַּׁבָּת הַגָּדוֹל וְהַקָּדוֹשׁ הַזֶּה כִּי יוֹם
זֶה גָּדוֹל וְקָדוֹשׁ הוּא לְפָנֶיךָ, לִשְׁבָּת בּוֹ וְלָנוּחַ בּוֹ
בְּאַהֲבָה כְּמִצְוַת רְצוֹנֶךָ, וּבִרְצוֹנְךָ הָנִיחַ לָנוּ יְיָ
אֱלֹהֵינוּ שֶׁלֹּא תְהֵא צָרָה וְיָגוֹן וַאֲנָחָה בְּיוֹם מְנוּחָתֵנוּ,
וְהַרְאֵנוּ יְיָ אֱלֹהֵינוּ בְּנֶחָמַת צִיּוֹן עִירֶךָ, וּבְבִנְיַן
יְרוּשָׁלַיִם עִיר קָדְשֶׁךָ, כִּי אַתָּה הוּא בַּעַל הַיְשׁוּעוֹת
וּבַעַל הַנֶּחָמוֹת:

The leader says the phrases from זָכְרֵנוּ to טוֹבִים aloud, and the others respond אָמֵן as indicated.

אֱלֹהֵינוּ וֵאלֹהֵי אֲבוֹתֵינוּ, יַעֲלֶה וְיָבוֹא וְיַגִּיעַ,
וְיֵרָאֶה וְיֵרָצֶה וְיִשָּׁמַע, וְיִפָּקֵד וְיִזָּכֵר

וְעַל For all this, GOD, our God, we thank You and bless You. May Your Name be blessed by the mouth of every living being, constantly and forever. As it is written: "When you have eaten and are satiated, you shall bless GOD, your God, for the good land which He has given you." Blessed are You, GOD, for the land and for the food.

רחם Have mercy, GOD, our God, upon Israel Your people, upon Jerusalem Your city, upon Zion the abode of Your glory, upon the kingship of the house of David Your anointed, and upon the great and holy House which is called by Your Name. Our God, our Father, our Shepherd, feed us, sustain us, nourish us and give us comfort; and speedily, GOD, our God, grant us relief from all our afflictions. GOD, our God, please do not make us dependent upon the gifts of mortal men nor upon their loans, but only upon Your full, open, holy and generous hand, that we may not be shamed or disgraced forever and ever.

On Friday night:

רצה May it please You, GOD, our God, to strengthen us through Your commandments, and through the precept of the Seventh Day, this great and holy Shabbat. For this day is great and holy before You, to refrain from work and to rest thereon with love, in accordance with the commandment of Your will. In Your will, GOD, our God, bestow upon us tranquility, that there shall be no trouble, sadness or grief on the day of our rest. GOD, our God, let us see the consolation of Zion Your city, and the rebuilding of Jerusalem Your holy city, for You are the Master of [all] salvations and the Master of [all] consolations.

The leader says the phrases from *Remember us* to *good life* aloud, and the others respond Amen as indicated.

אלהינו Our God and God of our fathers, may there ascend, come and reach, be seen, accepted and heard, recalled and remembered before You, the remembrance

זִכְרוֹנֵנוּ וּפִקְדוֹנֵנוּ, וְזִכְרוֹן אֲבוֹתֵינוּ, וְזִכְרוֹן מָשִׁיחַ בֶּן
דָּוִד עַבְדֶּךָ, וְזִכְרוֹן יְרוּשָׁלַיִם עִיר קָדְשֶׁךָ, וְזִכְרוֹן כָּל
עַמְּךָ בֵּית יִשְׂרָאֵל לְפָנֶיךָ, לִפְלֵיטָה לְטוֹבָה, לְחֵן
וּלְחֶסֶד וּלְרַחֲמִים וּלְחַיִּים טוֹבִים וּלְשָׁלוֹם, בְּיוֹם חַג
הַמַּצּוֹת הַזֶּה, בְּיוֹם טוֹב מִקְרָא קֹדֶשׁ הַזֶּה, זָכְרֵנוּ
יְיָ אֱלֹהֵינוּ בּוֹ לְטוֹבָה (אָמֵן), וּפָקְדֵנוּ בוֹ לִבְרָכָה
(אָמֵן), וְהוֹשִׁיעֵנוּ בוֹ לְחַיִּים טוֹבִים (אָמֵן), וּבִדְבַר
יְשׁוּעָה וְרַחֲמִים, חוּס וְחָנֵּנוּ, וְרַחֵם עָלֵינוּ וְהוֹשִׁיעֵנוּ,
כִּי אֵלֶיךָ עֵינֵינוּ, כִּי אֵל מֶלֶךְ חַנּוּן וְרַחוּם אָתָּה:

וּבְנֵה יְרוּשָׁלַיִם עִיר הַקֹּדֶשׁ בִּמְהֵרָה בְיָמֵינוּ. בָּרוּךְ
אַתָּה יְיָ, בֹּנֵה בְרַחֲמָיו יְרוּשָׁלָיִם. אָמֵן:

The cup is placed on the table.

בָּרוּךְ אַתָּה יְיָ, אֱלֹהֵינוּ מֶלֶךְ הָעוֹלָם, הָאֵל, אָבִינוּ
מַלְכֵּנוּ, אַדִּירֵנוּ בּוֹרְאֵנוּ גּוֹאֲלֵנוּ יוֹצְרֵנוּ,
קְדוֹשֵׁנוּ קְדוֹשׁ יַעֲקֹב, רוֹעֵנוּ רוֹעֵה יִשְׂרָאֵל הַמֶּלֶךְ
הַטּוֹב וְהַמֵּטִיב לַכֹּל בְּכָל יוֹם וָיוֹם, הוּא הֵטִיב לָנוּ,
הוּא מֵטִיב לָנוּ, הוּא יֵיטִיב לָנוּ, הוּא גְמָלָנוּ הוּא
גוֹמְלֵנוּ הוּא יִגְמְלֵנוּ לָעַד, לְחֵן וּלְחֶסֶד וּלְרַחֲמִים,
וּלְרֶוַח הַצָּלָה וְהַצְלָחָה, בְּרָכָה וִישׁוּעָה, נֶחָמָה פַּרְנָסָה
וְכַלְכָּלָה וְרַחֲמִים וְחַיִּים וְשָׁלוֹם וְכָל טוֹב וּמִכָּל
טוֹב לְעוֹלָם אַל יְחַסְּרֵנוּ: הָרַחֲמָן הוּא יִמְלוֹךְ עָלֵינוּ
לְעוֹלָם וָעֶד: הָרַחֲמָן הוּא יִתְבָּרֵךְ בַּשָּׁמַיִם וּבָאָרֶץ:
הָרַחֲמָן הוּא יִשְׁתַּבַּח לְדוֹר דּוֹרִים וְיִתְפָּאַר בָּנוּ לָעַד
וּלְנֵצַח נְצָחִים וְיִתְהַדַּר בָּנוּ לָעַד וּלְעוֹלְמֵי עוֹלָמִים:
הָרַחֲמָן הוּא יְפַרְנְסֵנוּ בְּכָבוֹד: הָרַחֲמָן הוּא יִשְׁבֹּר

and recollection of us, the remembrance of our fathers,
the remembrance of Moshiach the son of David Your
servant, the remembrance of Jerusalem Your holy city,
and the remembrance of Your entire people, the House
of Israel, for deliverance, well-being, grace, kindness,
mercy, good life and peace, on this day of the Festival
of Matzot, on this Festival of holy convocation. Remember us on it, GOD, our God, for good (Amen);
recollect us on it for blessing (Amen); help us on it for
good life (Amen). With the matter of salvation and
compassion, spare us and be gracious to us; have mercy
upon us and deliver us; for our eyes are directed to You,
for You, God, are a gracious and merciful King.

ובנה Rebuild Jerusalem the holy city speedily in our
days. Blessed are You, GOD, who in His mercy rebuilds
Jerusalem. Amen.

The cup is placed on the table.

ברוך Blessed are You, GOD, our God, King of the
universe, benevolent God, our Father, our King, our
Might, our Creator, our Redeemer, our Maker, our
Holy One, the Holy One of Jacob, our Shepherd, the
Shepherd of Israel, the King who is good and does good
to all, each and every day. He has done good for us, He
does good for us, and He will do good for us; He has
bestowed, He bestows, and He will forever bestow upon
us grace, kindness and mercy, relief, salvation and
success, blessing and help, consolation, sustenance and
nourishment, compassion, life, peace and all goodness;
and may He never cause us to lack any good. May the
Merciful One reign over us forever and ever. May the
Merciful One be blessed in heaven and on earth. May
the Merciful One be praised for all generations, and be
glorified in us forever and all eternity, and honored in
us forever and ever. May the Merciful One sustain us
with honor. May the Merciful One break the yoke of

עֹל גָּלוּת מֵעַל צַוָּארֵנוּ וְהוּא יוֹלִיכֵנוּ קוֹמְמִיּוּת
לְאַרְצֵנוּ: הָרַחֲמָן הוּא יִשְׁלַח בְּרָכָה מְרֻבָּה בְּבַיִת
זֶה וְעַל שֻׁלְחָן זֶה שֶׁאָכַלְנוּ עָלָיו: הָרַחֲמָן הוּא
יִשְׁלַח לָנוּ אֶת אֵלִיָּהוּ הַנָּבִיא זָכוּר לַטּוֹב וִיבַשֶּׂר
לָנוּ בְּשׂוֹרוֹת טוֹבוֹת יְשׁוּעוֹת וְנֶחָמוֹת: הָרַחֲמָן הוּא
יְבָרֵךְ אֶת אָבִי מוֹרִי בַּעַל הַבַּיִת הַזֶּה וְאֶת אִמִּי
מוֹרָתִי בַּעֲלַת הַבַּיִת הַזֶּה אוֹתָם וְאֶת בֵּיתָם וְאֶת
זַרְעָם וְאֶת כָּל אֲשֶׁר לָהֶם אוֹתָנוּ וְאֶת כָּל אֲשֶׁר
לָנוּ: כְּמוֹ שֶׁבֵּרַךְ אֶת אֲבוֹתֵינוּ אַבְרָהָם יִצְחָק וְיַעֲקֹב
בַּכֹּל מִכֹּל כֹּל, כֵּן יְבָרֵךְ אוֹתָנוּ (בְּנֵי בְרִית) כֻּלָּנוּ יַחַד
בִּבְרָכָה שְׁלֵמָה וְנֹאמַר אָמֵן:

מִמָּרוֹם יְלַמְּדוּ עָלָיו וְעָלֵינוּ זְכוּת שֶׁתְּהֵא
לְמִשְׁמֶרֶת שָׁלוֹם וְנִשָּׂא בְרָכָה מֵאֵת יְיָ
וּצְדָקָה מֵאֱלֹהֵי יִשְׁעֵנוּ וְנִמְצָא חֵן וְשֵׂכֶל טוֹב בְּעֵינֵי
אֱלֹהִים וְאָדָם:

On Friday night:

הָרַחֲמָן הוּא יַנְחִילֵנוּ לְיוֹם שֶׁכֻּלּוֹ שַׁבָּת וּמְנוּחָה לְחַיֵּי
הָעוֹלָמִים:

הָרַחֲמָן הוּא יַנְחִילֵנוּ לְיוֹם שֶׁכֻּלּוֹ טוֹב:

הָרַחֲמָן הוּא יְזַכֵּנוּ לִימוֹת הַמָּשִׁיחַ וּלְחַיֵּי הָעוֹלָם
הַבָּא. מִגְדּוֹל יְשׁוּעוֹת מַלְכּוֹ וְעֹשֶׂה חֶסֶד
לִמְשִׁיחוֹ לְדָוִד וּלְזַרְעוֹ עַד עוֹלָם: עֹשֶׂה שָׁלוֹם
בִּמְרוֹמָיו הוּא יַעֲשֶׂה שָׁלוֹם עָלֵינוּ וְעַל כָּל יִשְׂרָאֵל
וְאִמְרוּ אָמֵן:

exile from our neck, and may He lead us upright to our land. May the Merciful One send abundant blessing into this house and upon this table at which we have eaten. May the Merciful One send us Elijah the prophet—may he be remembered for good—and may he bring us good tidings, salvations and consolations. May the Merciful One bless my father, my teacher, the master of this house, and my mother, my teacher, the mistress of this house; them, their household, their children, and all that is theirs; us, and all that is ours. Just as He blessed our forefathers, Abraham, Isaac and Jacob, "in everything," "from everything," with "everything," so may He bless all of us (the children of the Covenant) together with a perfect blessing, and let us say, Amen.

ממרום From On High, may there be invoked upon him and upon us such merit which will bring a safeguarding of peace. May we receive blessing from GOD and just kindness from the God of our salvation, and may we find grace and good understanding in the eyes of God and man.

> On Friday night:
> הרחמן May the Merciful One cause us to inherit that day which will be all Shabbat and rest for life everlasting.

הרחמן May the Merciful One cause us to inherit that day which is all good.

הרחמן May the Merciful One grant us the privilege of reaching the days of Moshiach and the life of the World to Come. He is a tower of salvation to His king, and bestows kindness upon His anointed, to David and his descendants forever. He who makes peace in His heights, may He make peace for us and for all Israel; and say, Amen.

יְראוּ אֶת יְיָ קְדֹשָׁיו, כִּי אֵין מַחְסוֹר לִירֵאָיו:
כְּפִירִים רָשׁוּ וְרָעֵבוּ, וְדֹרְשֵׁי יְיָ לֹא יַחְסְרוּ
כָל טוֹב: הוֹדוּ לַיְיָ כִּי טוֹב, כִּי לְעוֹלָם חַסְדּוֹ: פּוֹתֵחַ
אֶת יָדֶךָ, וּמַשְׂבִּיעַ לְכָל חַי רָצוֹן: בָּרוּךְ הַגֶּבֶר אֲשֶׁר
יִבְטַח בַּיְיָ, וְהָיָה יְיָ מִבְטַחוֹ:

ומברך על הכוס ושותה בהסיבה
The cup is held in the palm of the right hand for the following blessing.

בָּרוּךְ אַתָּה יְיָ, אֱלֹהֵינוּ מֶלֶךְ הָעוֹלָם, בּוֹרֵא פְּרִי הַגָּפֶן:

Drink the entire cup without pause while seated, reclining on the left side. (One who cannot drink the entire cup should drink at least most of it.)

מוזגין כום ד' ופותחין הדלת ואומר:
The fourth cup is poured.

All doors between where the Seder is being conducted and the outside are opened, and the following paragraph is recited.

Those sent to open the doors recite the paragraph at the front door. On weeknights, it is customary to take a lit candle to the front door.

שְׁפוֹךְ חֲמָתְךָ אֶל הַגּוֹיִם אֲשֶׁר לֹא יְדָעוּךָ, וְעַל
מַמְלָכוֹת אֲשֶׁר בְּשִׁמְךָ לֹא קָרָאוּ: כִּי
אָכַל אֶת יַעֲקֹב, וְאֶת נָוֵהוּ הֵשַׁמּוּ: שְׁפָךְ עֲלֵיהֶם
זַעְמֶךָ וַחֲרוֹן אַפְּךָ יַשִּׂיגֵם: תִּרְדֹּף בְּאַף
וְתַשְׁמִידֵם מִתַּחַת שְׁמֵי יְיָ:

The doors are closed. When those sent to open the doors return, continue below.

הלל נרצה

לֹא לָנוּ יְיָ, לֹא לָנוּ, כִּי לְשִׁמְךָ תֵּן כָּבוֹד, עַל
חַסְדְּךָ עַל אֲמִתֶּךָ: לָמָּה יֹאמְרוּ הַגּוֹיִם, אַיֵּה

יראו Fear GOD, you His holy ones, for those who fear Him suffer no want. Young lions are in need and go hungry, but those who seek GOD shall not lack any good. Give thanks to GOD, for He is good, for His kindness is everlasting. You open Your hand and satisfy the desire of every living thing. Blessed is the man who trusts in GOD, and GOD will be his trust.

The cup is held in the palm of the right hand for the following blessing.

ברוך Blessed are You, GOD, our God, King of the universe, who creates the fruit of the vine.

Drink the entire cup without pause while seated, reclining on the left side. (One who cannot drink the entire cup should drink at least most of it.)

The fourth cup is poured.

All doors between where the Seder is being conducted and the outside are opened, and the following paragraph is recited.

Those sent to open the doors recite the paragraph at the front door. On weeknights, it is customary to take a lit candle to the front door.

שפוך Pour out Your wrath upon the nations that do not acknowledge You, and upon the kingdoms that do not call upon Your Name. For they have devoured Jacob and laid waste his habitation. Pour out Your indignation upon them, and let the wrath of Your anger overtake them. Pursue them with anger, and destroy them from beneath the heavens of GOD.

The doors are closed. When those sent to open the doors return, continue below.

Hallel Nirtzah

לא Not to us, GOD, not to us, but to Your Name give glory, for the sake of Your kindness and Your truth. Why should the nations say, "Where, now, is their

נָא אֱלֹהֵיהֶם: וֵאלֹהֵינוּ בַשָּׁמַיִם, כֹּל אֲשֶׁר חָפֵץ
עָשָׂה: עֲצַבֵּיהֶם כֶּסֶף וְזָהָב, מַעֲשֵׂה יְדֵי אָדָם: פֶּה
לָהֶם וְלֹא יְדַבֵּרוּ, עֵינַיִם לָהֶם וְלֹא יִרְאוּ: אָזְנַיִם
לָהֶם וְלֹא יִשְׁמָעוּ, אַף לָהֶם וְלֹא יְרִיחוּן: יְדֵיהֶם
וְלֹא יְמִישׁוּן, רַגְלֵיהֶם וְלֹא יְהַלֵּכוּ, לֹא יֶהְגּוּ בִּגְרוֹנָם:
כְּמוֹהֶם יִהְיוּ עֹשֵׂיהֶם, כֹּל אֲשֶׁר בֹּטֵחַ בָּהֶם: יִשְׂרָאֵל
בְּטַח בַּיָי, עֶזְרָם וּמָגִנָּם הוּא: בֵּית אַהֲרֹן בִּטְחוּ בַיָי,
עֶזְרָם וּמָגִנָּם הוּא: יִרְאֵי יְיָ בִּטְחוּ בַיָי, עֶזְרָם וּמָגִנָּם
הוּא:

יְיָ זְכָרָנוּ יְבָרֵךְ, יְבָרֵךְ אֶת בֵּית יִשְׂרָאֵל, יְבָרֵךְ אֶת
בֵּית אַהֲרֹן: יְבָרֵךְ יִרְאֵי יְיָ, הַקְּטַנִּים עִם
הַגְּדֹלִים: יֹסֵף יְיָ עֲלֵיכֶם, עֲלֵיכֶם וְעַל בְּנֵיכֶם:
בְּרוּכִים אַתֶּם לַיָי, עֹשֵׂה שָׁמַיִם וָאָרֶץ: הַשָּׁמַיִם
שָׁמַיִם לַיָי, וְהָאָרֶץ נָתַן לִבְנֵי אָדָם: לֹא הַמֵּתִים
יְהַלְלוּ יָהּ, וְלֹא כָּל יֹרְדֵי דוּמָה: וַאֲנַחְנוּ נְבָרֵךְ יָהּ,
מֵעַתָּה וְעַד עוֹלָם, הַלְלוּיָהּ:

אָהַבְתִּי, כִּי יִשְׁמַע יְיָ אֶת קוֹלִי תַּחֲנוּנָי: כִּי הִטָּה
אָזְנוֹ לִי, וּבְיָמַי אֶקְרָא: אֲפָפוּנִי חֶבְלֵי
מָוֶת, וּמְצָרֵי שְׁאוֹל מְצָאוּנִי, צָרָה וְיָגוֹן אֶמְצָא:
וּבְשֵׁם יְיָ אֶקְרָא, אָנָּה יְיָ מַלְּטָה נַפְשִׁי: חַנּוּן יְיָ
וְצַדִּיק, וֵאלֹהֵינוּ מְרַחֵם: שֹׁמֵר פְּתָאיִם יְיָ, דַּלוֹתִי וְלִי
יְהוֹשִׁיעַ: שׁוּבִי נַפְשִׁי לִמְנוּחָיְכִי, כִּי יְיָ גָּמַל עָלָיְכִי:
כִּי חִלַּצְתָּ נַפְשִׁי מִמָּוֶת, אֶת עֵינִי מִן דִּמְעָה, אֶת
רַגְלִי מִדֶּחִי: אֶתְהַלֵּךְ לִפְנֵי יְיָ, בְּאַרְצוֹת הַחַיִּים:

God?" Our God is in heaven, He does whatever He pleases. Their idols are of silver and gold, the product of human hands: they have a mouth, but cannot speak; they have eyes, but cannot see; they have ears, but cannot hear; they have a nose, but cannot smell; their hands cannot feel; their feet cannot walk; they can make no sound with their throat. Like them should be their makers, everyone that trusts in them. Israel, trust in GOD! He is their help and their shield. House of Aaron, trust in GOD! He is their help and their shield. You who fear GOD, trust in GOD! He is their help and their shield.

ʻʻ GOD, mindful of us, will bless. He will bless the House of Israel; He will bless the House of Aaron; He will bless those who fear GOD, the small with the great. May GOD increase [blessing] upon you, upon you and upon your children. You are blessed unto GOD, the Maker of heaven and earth. The heavens are the heavens of GOD, but the earth He gave to the children of man. The dead do not praise God, nor do those that go down into the silence [of the grave]. But we will bless God, from now to eternity. Halleluyah—Praise God!

אהבתי I love GOD, because He hears my voice, my prayers. For He turned His ear to me; all my days I will call [upon Him]. The pangs of death encompassed me, and the agonies of the grave came upon me, trouble and sorrow I encounter and I call upon the Name of GOD: "Please, GOD, deliver my soul!" GOD is gracious and just; our God is compassionate. GOD watches over the simpletons; I was brought low and He saved me. Return, my soul, to your rest, for GOD has dealt kindly with you. For You have delivered my soul from death, my eyes from tears, my foot from stumbling. I will walk before GOD in the lands of the living. I had faith even

הֶאֱמַנְתִּי כִּי אֲדַבֵּר, אֲנִי עָנִיתִי מְאֹד: אֲנִי אָמַרְתִּי
בְחָפְזִי, כָּל הָאָדָם כֹּזֵב:

מָה אָשִׁיב לַיָי, כָּל תַּגְמוּלוֹהִי עָלָי: כּוֹס יְשׁוּעוֹת
אֶשָּׂא, וּבְשֵׁם יְיָ אֶקְרָא: נְדָרַי לַיָי אֲשַׁלֵּם,
נֶגְדָה נָּא לְכָל עַמּוֹ: יָקָר בְּעֵינֵי יְיָ, הַמָּוְתָה
לַחֲסִידָיו: אָנָּה יְיָ כִּי אֲנִי עַבְדֶּךָ, אֲנִי עַבְדְּךָ בֶּן
אֲמָתֶךָ, פִּתַּחְתָּ לְמוֹסֵרָי: לְךָ אֶזְבַּח זֶבַח תּוֹדָה,
וּבְשֵׁם יְיָ אֶקְרָא: נְדָרַי לַיָי אֲשַׁלֵּם, נֶגְדָה נָּא לְכָל
עַמּוֹ: בְּחַצְרוֹת בֵּית יְיָ, בְּתוֹכֵכִי יְרוּשָׁלָיִם,
הַלְלוּיָהּ:

הַלְלוּ אֶת יְיָ כָּל גּוֹיִם, שַׁבְּחוּהוּ כָּל הָאֻמִּים: כִּי
גָבַר עָלֵינוּ חַסְדּוֹ, וֶאֱמֶת יְיָ לְעוֹלָם,
הַלְלוּיָהּ:

The four verses in larger type are recited aloud by the leader. After each verse, all others respond הוֹדוּ לַיָי כִּי טוֹב כִּי לְעוֹלָם חַסְדּוֹ, and then recite the subsequent verse in an undertone as indicated. (The leader recites הוֹדוּ after each of the last three verses.)

—Leader	**הוֹדוּ לַיָי כִּי טוֹב,** כִּי לְעוֹלָם חַסְדּוֹ:
—All others	הוֹדוּ לַיָי כִּי טוֹב, כִּי לְעוֹלָם חַסְדּוֹ:
	יֹאמַר נָא יִשְׂרָאֵל, כִּי לְעוֹלָם חַסְדּוֹ:
—Leader	**יֹאמַר נָא יִשְׂרָאֵל,** כִּי לְעוֹלָם חַסְדּוֹ:
—All others	הוֹדוּ לַיָי כִּי טוֹב, כִּי לְעוֹלָם חַסְדּוֹ:
	יֹאמְרוּ נָא בֵית אַהֲרֹן, כִּי לְעוֹלָם חַסְדּוֹ:
—Leader	**יֹאמְרוּ נָא בֵית אַהֲרֹן,** כִּי לְעוֹלָם חַסְדּוֹ:
—All others	הוֹדוּ לַיָי כִּי טוֹב, כִּי לְעוֹלָם חַסְדּוֹ:
	יֹאמְרוּ נָא יִרְאֵי יְיָ, כִּי לְעוֹלָם חַסְדּוֹ:

when I said, "I am greatly afflicted"; [even when] I said in my haste, "All men are deceitful."

מה What can I repay GOD for all His kindness to me? I will raise the cup of salvation and call upon the Name of GOD. I will pay my vows to GOD, now, in the presence of all His people. Precious in the eyes of GOD is the death of His pious ones. I thank you, GOD, for I am Your servant. I am Your servant the son of Your handmaid; You have loosened my bonds. To You I will bring an offering of thanksgiving, and I will call upon the Name of GOD. I will pay my vows to GOD, now, in the presence of all His people, in the courtyards of the House of GOD, in the midst of Jerusalem. Halleluyah—Praise God!

הללו Praise GOD, all nations! Extol Him, all peoples! For His kindness was mighty over us, and the truth of GOD is everlasting. Halleluyah—Praise God!

The four verses in larger type are recited aloud by the leader. After each verse, all others respond *Give thanks to GOD, for He is good, for His kindness is everlasting,* and then recite the subsequent verse in an undertone as indicated. (The leader recites *Give thanks* after each of the last three verses.)

Leader—הודו **Give thanks to GOD, for He is good, for His kindness is everlasting.**

All others—הודו Give thanks to GOD, for He is good, for His kindness is everlasting.

יאמר Let Israel say [it], for His kindness is everlasting.

Leader—יאמר **Let Israel say [it], for His kindness is everlasting.**

All others—Give thanks to GOD, for He is good, for His kindness is everlasting.

יאמרו Let the House of Aaron say [it], for His kindness is everlasting.

Leader—יאמרו **Let the House of Aaron say [it], for His kindness is everlasting.**

All others—Give thanks to GOD, for He is good, for His kindness is everlasting.

יאמרו Let those who fear GOD say [it], for His kindness is everlasting.

Leader—יֹאמְרוּ נָא יִרְאֵי יְיָ,   כִּי לְעוֹלָם חַסְדּוֹ:

All others—הוֹדוּ לַיְיָ כִּי טוֹב,   כִּי לְעוֹלָם חַסְדּוֹ:

מִן הַמֵּצַר קָרָאתִי יָּהּ, עָנָנִי בַמֶּרְחָב יָהּ: יְיָ לִי לֹא
אִירָא, מַה יַּעֲשֶׂה לִי אָדָם: יְיָ לִי בְּעֹזְרָי, וַאֲנִי
אֶרְאֶה בְשֹׂנְאָי: טוֹב לַחֲסוֹת בַּיְיָ, מִבְּטֹחַ בָּאָדָם: טוֹב
לַחֲסוֹת בַּיְיָ, מִבְּטֹחַ בִּנְדִיבִים: כָּל גּוֹיִם סְבָבוּנִי, בְּשֵׁם
יְיָ כִּי אֲמִילַם: סַבּוּנִי גַם סְבָבוּנִי, בְּשֵׁם יְיָ כִּי אֲמִילַם:
סַבּוּנִי כִדְבֹרִים דֹּעֲכוּ כְּאֵשׁ קוֹצִים, בְּשֵׁם יְיָ כִּי
אֲמִילַם: דָּחֹה דְחִיתַנִי לִנְפֹּל, וַיְיָ עֲזָרָנִי: עָזִּי וְזִמְרָת יָהּ,
וַיְהִי לִי לִישׁוּעָה: קוֹל רִנָּה וִישׁוּעָה בְּאָהֳלֵי צַדִּיקִים,
יְמִין יְיָ עֹשָׂה חָיִל: יְמִין יְיָ רוֹמֵמָה, יְמִין יְיָ עֹשָׂה חָיִל:
לֹא אָמוּת כִּי אֶחְיֶה, וַאֲסַפֵּר מַעֲשֵׂי יָהּ: יַסֹּר יִסְּרַנִּי יָּהּ,
וְלַמָּוֶת לֹא נְתָנָנִי: פִּתְחוּ לִי שַׁעֲרֵי צֶדֶק, אָבֹא בָם
אוֹדֶה יָהּ: זֶה הַשַּׁעַר לַיְיָ, צַדִּיקִים יָבֹאוּ בוֹ: אוֹדְךָ כִּי
עֲנִיתָנִי, וַתְּהִי לִי לִישׁוּעָה: אוֹדְךָ כִּי עֲנִיתָנִי, וַתְּהִי לִי
לִישׁוּעָה: אֶבֶן מָאֲסוּ הַבּוֹנִים, הָיְתָה לְרֹאשׁ פִּנָּה: אֶבֶן
מָאֲסוּ הַבּוֹנִים, הָיְתָה לְרֹאשׁ פִּנָּה: מֵאֵת יְיָ הָיְתָה
זֹּאת, הִיא נִפְלָאת בְּעֵינֵינוּ: מֵאֵת יְיָ הָיְתָה זֹּאת, הִיא
נִפְלָאת בְּעֵינֵינוּ: זֶה הַיּוֹם עָשָׂה יְיָ, נָגִילָה וְנִשְׂמְחָה
בוֹ: זֶה הַיּוֹם עָשָׂה יְיָ, נָגִילָה וְנִשְׂמְחָה בוֹ:

Each of the following four lines is recited aloud by the leader, followed by all others.

אָנָּא יְיָ הוֹשִׁיעָה נָּא:

אָנָּא יְיָ הוֹשִׁיעָה נָּא:

אָנָּא יְיָ הַצְלִיחָה נָּא:

אָנָּא יְיָ הַצְלִיחָה נָּא:

Leader—יאמרו **Let those who fear GOD say [it],**
for His kindness is everlasting.

All others—Give thanks to GOD, for He is good,
for His kindness is everlasting.

מן Out of narrow confines I called to God; God answered me with abounding relief. GOD is with me, I will not fear—what can man do to me? GOD is with me, through my helpers, and I can face my enemies. It is better to rely on GOD, than to trust in man. It is better to rely on GOD, than to trust in nobles. All nations surround me, but I cut them down in the Name of GOD. They surrounded me, they encompassed me, but I cut them down in the Name of GOD. They surrounded me like bees, yet they are extinguished like a fire of thorns; I cut them down in the Name of GOD. You [my foes] pushed me again and again to fall, but GOD helped me. God is my strength and song, and this has been my salvation. The sound of joyous song and salvation is in the tents of the righteous: "The right hand of GOD performs deeds of valor. The right hand of GOD is exalted; the right hand of GOD performs deeds of valor!" I shall not die, but I shall live and relate the deeds of God. God has chastised me, but He did not give me over to death. Open for me the gates of righteousness; I will enter them and give thanks to God. This is the gate of GOD, the righteous will enter it. I thank You, for You have answered me, and You have been a help to me. I thank You, for You have answered me, and You have been a help to me. The stone scorned by the builders has become the main cornerstone. The stone scorned by the builders has become the main cornerstone. This was indeed from GOD; it is wondrous in our eyes. This was indeed from GOD; it is wondrous in our eyes. This day GOD has made; let us be glad and rejoice on it. This day GOD has made; let us be glad and rejoice on it.

Each of the following four lines is recited aloud by the leader, followed by all others.

אנא **We implore You, GOD, deliver us now.**

אנא **We implore You, GOD, deliver us now.**

אנא **We implore You, GOD, grant us success now.**

אנא **We implore You, GOD, grant us success now.**

בָּרוּךְ הַבָּא בְּשֵׁם יְיָ, בֵּרַכְנוּכֶם מִבֵּית יְיָ: בָּרוּךְ
הַבָּא בְּשֵׁם יְיָ, בֵּרַכְנוּכֶם מִבֵּית יְיָ: אֵל יְיָ
וַיָּאֶר לָנוּ, אִסְרוּ חַג בַּעֲבֹתִים, עַד קַרְנוֹת הַמִּזְבֵּחַ:
אֵל יְיָ וַיָּאֶר לָנוּ, אִסְרוּ חַג בַּעֲבֹתִים, עַד קַרְנוֹת
הַמִּזְבֵּחַ: אֵלִי אַתָּה וְאוֹדֶךָּ, אֱלֹהַי אֲרוֹמְמֶךָּ: אֵלִי
אַתָּה וְאוֹדֶךָּ, אֱלֹהַי אֲרוֹמְמֶךָּ: הוֹדוּ לַיְיָ כִּי טוֹב,
כִּי לְעוֹלָם חַסְדּוֹ: הוֹדוּ לַיְיָ כִּי טוֹב, כִּי לְעוֹלָם
חַסְדּוֹ:

יְהַלְלוּךָ יְיָ אֱלֹהֵינוּ (עַל) כָּל מַעֲשֶׂיךָ, וַחֲסִידֶיךָ
צַדִּיקִים עוֹשֵׂי רְצוֹנֶךָ, וְכָל עַמְּךָ בֵּית
יִשְׂרָאֵל, בְּרִנָּה יוֹדוּ וִיבָרְכוּ, וִישַׁבְּחוּ וִיפָאֲרוּ,
וִירוֹמְמוּ וְיַעֲרִיצוּ, וְיַקְדִּישׁוּ וְיַמְלִיכוּ אֶת שִׁמְךָ
מַלְכֵּנוּ. כִּי לְךָ טוֹב לְהוֹדוֹת, וּלְשִׁמְךָ נָאֶה לְזַמֵּר,
כִּי מֵעוֹלָם וְעַד עוֹלָם אַתָּה אֵל:

There are twenty-six verses in this Psalm, coresponding to the numerical equivalent of the Tetragrammaton. When saying the first ten verses, one should have in mind (but not articulate) the letter י of the Tetragrammaton; for the next five verses, have in mind the letter ה of the Tetragrammaton; for the next six verses, the letter ו of the Tetragrammaton; and for the last five verses, the second ה of the Tetragrammaton.

כִּי לְעוֹלָם חַסְדּוֹ:	הוֹדוּ לַיְיָ כִּי טוֹב,
כִּי לְעוֹלָם חַסְדּוֹ:	הוֹדוּ לֵאלֹהֵי הָאֱלֹהִים,
כִּי לְעוֹלָם חַסְדּוֹ:	הוֹדוּ לַאֲדֹנֵי הָאֲדֹנִים,
כִּי לְעוֹלָם חַסְדּוֹ:	לְעוֹשֵׂה נִפְלָאוֹת גְּדֹלוֹת לְבַדּוֹ,
כִּי לְעוֹלָם חַסְדּוֹ:	לְעוֹשֵׂה הַשָּׁמַיִם בִּתְבוּנָה,
כִּי לְעוֹלָם חַסְדּוֹ:	לְרוֹקַע הָאָרֶץ עַל הַמָּיִם,

ברוך Blessed is he who comes in the Name of GOD; we bless you from the House of GOD. Blessed is he who comes in the Name of GOD; we bless you from the House of GOD. GOD is Almighty, He gave us light; bind the festival-offering with cords until [you bring it to] the horns of the altar. GOD is Almighty, He gave us light; bind the festival-offering with cords until [you bring it to] the horns of the altar. You are my God and I will thank You; my God, I will exalt You. You are my God and I will thank You; my God, I will exalt You. Give thanks to GOD, for He is good, for His kindness is everlasting. Give thanks to GOD, for He is good, for His kindness is everlasting.

יהללוך GOD, our God, all Your works shall praise You; Your pious ones, the righteous who do Your will, and all Your people, the House of Israel, with joyous song will thank and bless, laud and glorify, exalt and adore, sanctify and proclaim the sovereignty of Your Name, our King. For it is good to thank You, and befitting to sing to Your Name, for from the beginning to the end of the world You are Almighty God.

There are twenty-six verses in this Psalm, coresponding to the numerical equivalent of the Tetragrammaton. When saying the first ten verses, one should have in mind (but not articulate) the letter י of the Tetragrammaton; for the next five verses, have in mind the letter ה of the Tetragrammaton; for the next six verses, the letter ו of the Tetragrammaton; and for the last five verses, the second ה of the Tetragrammaton.

הודו Give thanks to GOD, for He is good,

> for His kindness is everlasting;

Give thanks to the God of gods,

> for His kindness is everlasting;

Give thanks to the Lord of lords,

> for His kindness is everlasting;

Who alone does great wonders,

> for His kindness is everlasting;

Who made the heavens with understanding,

> for His kindness is everlasting;

Who stretched out the earth above the waters,

> for His kindness is everlasting;

הגדה של
פסח

לְעֹשֵׂה אוֹרִים גְּדֹלִים, כִּי לְעוֹלָם חַסְדּוֹ:

אֶת הַשֶּׁמֶשׁ לְמֶמְשֶׁלֶת בַּיּוֹם, כִּי לְעוֹלָם חַסְדּוֹ:

אֶת הַיָּרֵחַ וְכוֹכָבִים לְמֶמְשְׁלוֹת בַּלָּיְלָה,

כִּי לְעוֹלָם חַסְדּוֹ:

לְמַכֵּה מִצְרַיִם בִּבְכוֹרֵיהֶם, (ז) כִּי לְעוֹלָם חַסְדּוֹ:

וַיּוֹצֵא יִשְׂרָאֵל מִתּוֹכָם, כִּי לְעוֹלָם חַסְדּוֹ:

בְּיָד חֲזָקָה וּבִזְרוֹעַ נְטוּיָה, כִּי לְעוֹלָם חַסְדּוֹ:

לְגֹזֵר יַם סוּף לִגְזָרִים, כִּי לְעוֹלָם חַסְדּוֹ:

וְהֶעֱבִיר יִשְׂרָאֵל בְּתוֹכוֹ, כִּי לְעוֹלָם חַסְדּוֹ:

וְנִעֵר פַּרְעֹה וְחֵילוֹ בְיַם סוּף, (ה) כִּי לְעוֹלָם חַסְדּוֹ:

לְמוֹלִיךְ עַמּוֹ בַּמִּדְבָּר, כִּי לְעוֹלָם חַסְדּוֹ:

לְמַכֵּה מְלָכִים גְּדֹלִים, כִּי לְעוֹלָם חַסְדּוֹ:

וַיַּהֲרֹג מְלָכִים אַדִּירִים, כִּי לְעוֹלָם חַסְדּוֹ:

לְסִיחוֹן מֶלֶךְ הָאֱמֹרִי, כִּי לְעוֹלָם חַסְדּוֹ:

וּלְעוֹג מֶלֶךְ הַבָּשָׁן, כִּי לְעוֹלָם חַסְדּוֹ:

וְנָתַן אַרְצָם לְנַחֲלָה, (ו) כִּי לְעוֹלָם חַסְדּוֹ:

נַחֲלָה לְיִשְׂרָאֵל עַבְדּוֹ, כִּי לְעוֹלָם חַסְדּוֹ:

שֶׁבְּשִׁפְלֵנוּ זָכַר לָנוּ, כִּי לְעוֹלָם חַסְדּוֹ:

וַיִּפְרְקֵנוּ מִצָּרֵינוּ, כִּי לְעוֹלָם חַסְדּוֹ:

נֹתֵן לֶחֶם לְכָל בָּשָׂר, כִּי לְעוֹלָם חַסְדּוֹ:

הוֹדוּ לְאֵל הַשָּׁמָיִם, (ה) כִּי לְעוֹלָם חַסְדּוֹ:

הלל
נרצה

Who made the great lights,

> for His kindness is everlasting;

The sun to rule by day,

> for His kindness is everlasting;

The moon and stars to rule by night,

> for His kindness is everlasting;

Who struck Egypt through their firstborn,

> (יָ) for His kindness is everlasting;

And brought Israel out of their midst,

> for His kindness is everlasting;

With a strong hand and with an outstretched arm,

> for His kindness is everlasting;

Who split the Sea of Reeds into sections,

> for His kindness is everlasting;

And led Israel through it,

> for His kindness is everlasting;

And cast Pharaoh and his army into the Sea of Reeds,

> (הָ) for His kindness is everlasting;

Who led His people through the desert,

> for His kindness is everlasting;

Who struck great kings,

> for His kindness is everlasting;

And slew mighty kings,

> for His kindness is everlasting;

Sichon, king of the Amorites,

> for His kindness is everlasting;

And Og, king of Bashan,

> for His kindness is everlasting;

And gave their land as a heritage,

> (וָ) for His kindness is everlasting;

A heritage to Israel, His servant,

> for His kindness is everlasting;

Who remembered us in our lowliness,

> for His kindness is everlasting;

And delivered us from our oppressors,

> for His kindness is everlasting;

Who gives food to all flesh,

> for His kindness is everlasting;

Thank the God of heaven,

> (הָ) for His kindness is everlasting;

נִשְׁמַת כָּל חַי תְּבָרֵךְ אֶת שִׁמְךָ יְיָ אֱלֹהֵינוּ, וְרוּחַ
כָּל בָּשָׂר תְּפָאֵר וּתְרוֹמֵם זִכְרְךָ מַלְכֵּנוּ
תָּמִיד, מִן הָעוֹלָם וְעַד הָעוֹלָם אַתָּה אֵל,
וּמִבַּלְעָדֶיךָ אֵין לָנוּ מֶלֶךְ גּוֹאֵל וּמוֹשִׁיעַ, פּוֹדֶה
וּמַצִּיל וּמְפַרְנֵס וְעוֹנֶה וּמְרַחֵם בְּכָל עֵת צָרָה
וְצוּקָה, אֵין לָנוּ מֶלֶךְ אֶלָּא אָתָּה, אֱלֹהֵי הָרִאשׁוֹנִים
וְהָאַחֲרוֹנִים. אֱלוֹהַּ כָּל בְּרִיּוֹת, אֲדוֹן כָּל תּוֹלָדוֹת,
הַמְהֻלָּל בְּרוֹב הַתִּשְׁבָּחוֹת, הַמְנַהֵג עוֹלָמוֹ בְּחֶסֶד
וּבְרִיּוֹתָיו בְּרַחֲמִים. וַיְיָ הִנֵּה לֹא יָנוּם וְלֹא יִישָׁן,
הַמְעוֹרֵר יְשֵׁנִים, וְהַמֵּקִיץ נִרְדָּמִים, וְהַמֵּשִׂיחַ אִלְּמִים,
וְהַמַּתִּיר אֲסוּרִים, וְהַסּוֹמֵךְ נוֹפְלִים, וְהַזּוֹקֵף כְּפוּפִים,
לְךָ לְבַדְּךָ אֲנַחְנוּ מוֹדִים. אִלּוּ פִינוּ מָלֵא שִׁירָה כַיָּם,
וּלְשׁוֹנֵנוּ רִנָּה כַּהֲמוֹן גַּלָּיו, וְשִׂפְתוֹתֵינוּ שֶׁבַח
כְּמֶרְחֲבֵי רָקִיעַ, וְעֵינֵינוּ מְאִירוֹת כַּשֶּׁמֶשׁ וְכַיָּרֵחַ,
וְיָדֵינוּ פְרוּשׂוֹת כְּנִשְׁרֵי שָׁמָיִם, וְרַגְלֵינוּ קַלּוֹת
כָּאַיָּלוֹת, אֵין אָנוּ מַסְפִּיקִים לְהוֹדוֹת לְךָ יְיָ אֱלֹהֵינוּ
וֵאלֹהֵי אֲבוֹתֵינוּ, וּלְבָרֵךְ אֶת שְׁמֶךָ עַל אַחַת מֵאֶלֶף
אַלְפֵי אֲלָפִים, וְרִבֵּי רְבָבוֹת פְּעָמִים, הַטּוֹבוֹת נִסִּים
וְנִפְלָאוֹת שֶׁעָשִׂיתָ עִמָּנוּ וְעִם אֲבוֹתֵינוּ מִלְּפָנִים:
מִמִּצְרַיִם גְּאַלְתָּנוּ, יְיָ אֱלֹהֵינוּ, מִבֵּית עֲבָדִים פְּדִיתָנוּ,
בְּרָעָב זַנְתָּנוּ, וּבְשָׂבָע כִּלְכַּלְתָּנוּ, מֵחֶרֶב הִצַּלְתָּנוּ,
וּמִדֶּבֶר מִלַּטְתָּנוּ, וּמֵחֳלָיִם רָעִים וְנֶאֱמָנִים דִּלִּיתָנוּ.
עַד הֵנָּה עֲזָרוּנוּ רַחֲמֶיךָ, וְלֹא עֲזָבוּנוּ חֲסָדֶיךָ, וְאַל
תִּטְּשֵׁנוּ יְיָ אֱלֹהֵינוּ, לָנֶצַח. עַל כֵּן, אֵבָרִים שֶׁפִּלַּגְתָּ

נשמת The soul of every living being shall bless Your Name, GOD, our God; and the spirit of all flesh shall always glorify and exalt Your remembrance, our King. From the beginning to the end of the world You are Almighty God; and other than You we have no King, Redeemer and Savior who delivers, rescues, sustains, answers and is merciful in every time of trouble and distress; we have no King but You. [You are] the God of the first and of the last [generations], God of all creatures, Lord of all events, who is extolled with manifold praises, who directs His world with kindness and His creatures with compassion. Behold, GOD neither slumbers nor sleeps. He arouses the sleepers and awakens the slumberers, gives speech to the mute, releases the bound, supports the falling and raises up those who are bowed. To You alone we give thanks. Even if our mouths were filled with song as the sea, and our tongues with joyous singing like the multitudes of its waves, and our lips with praise like the expanse of the sky; and our eyes were shining like the sun and the moon, and our hands spread out like the eagles of heaven, and our feet swift like deer—we would still be unable to thank You, GOD, our God and God of our fathers, and to bless Your Name, for even one of the thousands of millions, and myriads of myriads, of favors, miracles and wonders which You have done for us and for our fathers before us. GOD, our God, You have redeemed us from Egypt, You have freed us from the house of bondage, You have fed us in famine and nourished us in plenty; You have saved us from the sword and delivered us from pestilence, and raised us from evil and lasting maladies. Until now Your mercies have helped us, and Your kindnesses have not forsaken us; and do not abandon us, GOD our God, forever! Therefore, the limbs which You have arranged within

בָּנוּ, וְרוּחַ וּנְשָׁמָה שֶׁנָּפַחְתָּ בְּאַפֵּינוּ, וְלָשׁוֹן אֲשֶׁר
שַׂמְתָּ בְּפִינוּ. הֵן הֵם: יוֹדוּ וִיבָרְכוּ וִישַׁבְּחוּ וִיפָאֲרוּ,
וִירוֹמְמוּ וְיַעֲרִיצוּ, וְיַקְדִּישׁוּ וְיַמְלִיכוּ אֶת שִׁמְךָ
מַלְכֵּנוּ. כִּי כָל פֶּה לְךָ יוֹדֶה, וְכָל לָשׁוֹן לְךָ תִשָּׁבַע,
וְכָל עַיִן לְךָ תְצַפֶּה, וְכָל בֶּרֶךְ לְךָ תִכְרַע, וְכָל קוֹמָה
לְפָנֶיךָ תִשְׁתַּחֲוֶה, וְכָל הַלְּבָבוֹת יִירָאוּךָ, וְכָל קֶרֶב
וּכְלָיוֹת יְזַמְּרוּ לִשְׁמֶךָ, כַּדָּבָר שֶׁכָּתוּב: כָּל עַצְמוֹתַי
תֹּאמַרְנָה, יְיָ, מִי כָמוֹךָ, מַצִּיל עָנִי מֵחָזָק מִמֶּנּוּ, וְעָנִי
וְאֶבְיוֹן מִגֹּזְלוֹ: מִי יִדְמֶה לָּךְ, וּמִי יִשְׁוֶה לָּךְ, וּמִי
יַעֲרָךְ לָךְ, הָאֵל הַגָּדוֹל, הַגִּבּוֹר וְהַנּוֹרָא, אֵל עֶלְיוֹן,
קֹנֵה שָׁמַיִם וָאָרֶץ. נְהַלֶּלְךָ, וּנְשַׁבֵּחֲךָ, וּנְפָאֶרְךָ,
וּנְבָרֵךְ אֶת שֵׁם קָדְשֶׁךָ, כָּאָמוּר: לְדָוִד, בָּרְכִי נַפְשִׁי
אֶת יְיָ, וְכָל קְרָבַי אֶת שֵׁם קָדְשׁוֹ:

הָאֵל בְּתַעֲצֻמוֹת עֻזֶּךָ, הַגָּדוֹל בִּכְבוֹד שְׁמֶךָ,
הַגִּבּוֹר לָנֶצַח, וְהַנּוֹרָא בְּנוֹרְאוֹתֶיךָ, הַמֶּלֶךְ
הַיּוֹשֵׁב עַל כִּסֵּא רָם וְנִשָּׂא:

שׁוֹכֵן עַד, מָרוֹם וְקָדוֹשׁ שְׁמוֹ, וְכָתוּב: רַנְּנוּ
צַדִּיקִים בַּיְיָ, לַיְשָׁרִים נָאוָה תְהִלָּה: בְּפִי
יְשָׁרִים תִּתְרוֹמָם, וּבְשִׂפְתֵי צַדִּיקִים תִּתְבָּרַךְ, וּבִלְשׁוֹן
חֲסִידִים תִּתְקַדָּשׁ, וּבְקֶרֶב קְדוֹשִׁים תִּתְהַלָּל:

וּבְמַקְהֲלוֹת רִבְבוֹת עַמְּךָ בֵּית יִשְׂרָאֵל, בְּרִנָּה
יִתְפָּאֵר שִׁמְךָ מַלְכֵּנוּ בְּכָל דּוֹר
וָדוֹר. שֶׁכֵּן חוֹבַת כָּל הַיְצוּרִים, לְפָנֶיךָ יְיָ אֱלֹהֵינוּ

us, and the spirit and soul which You have breathed into our nostrils, and the tongue which You have placed in our mouth—they all shall thank, bless, praise, glorify, exalt, adore, sanctify and proclaim the sovereignty of Your Name, our King. For every mouth shall offer thanks to You, every tongue shall swear by You, every eye shall look to You, every knee shall bend to You, all who stand erect shall bow down before You, all hearts shall fear You, and every innermost part shall sing praise to Your Name, as it is written: "All my bones will say, GOD, who is like You; You save the poor from one stronger than he, the poor and the needy from one who would rob him!" Who can be likened to You, who is equal to You, who can be compared to You, the great, mighty, awesome God, God most high, Possessor of heaven and earth! We will laud You, praise You and glorify You, and we will bless Your holy Name, as it is said: "[A Psalm] by David; bless GOD, O my soul, and all that is within me, [bless] His holy Name."

האל You are the Almighty God in the power of Your strength; the Great in the glory of Your Name; the Mighty forever, and the Awesome in Your awesome deeds; the King who sits upon a lofty and exalted throne.

שוכן He who dwells for eternity, lofty and holy is His Name. And it is written: "Sing joyously to GOD, you righteous; it befits the upright to offer praise." By the mouth of the upright You are exalted; by the lips of the righteous You are blessed; by the tongue of the pious You are sanctified; and among the holy ones You are praised.

ובמקהלות In the assemblies of the myriads of Your people, the House of Israel, Your Name, our King, shall be glorified with song in every generation. For such is the obligation of all creatures before You, GOD, our

וֵאלֹהֵי אֲבוֹתֵינוּ: לְהוֹדוֹת, לְהַלֵּל, לְשַׁבֵּחַ, לְפָאֵר, לְרוֹמֵם, לְהַדֵּר, לְבָרֵךְ, לְעַלֵּה וּלְקַלֵּס, עַל כָּל דִּבְרֵי שִׁירוֹת וְתִשְׁבָּחוֹת דָּוִד בֶּן יִשַׁי עַבְדְּךָ מְשִׁיחֶךָ:

וּבְכֵן יִשְׁתַּבַּח שִׁמְךָ לָעַד מַלְכֵּנוּ, הָאֵל, הַמֶּלֶךְ הַגָּדוֹל וְהַקָּדוֹשׁ בַּשָּׁמַיִם וּבָאָרֶץ. כִּי לְךָ נָאֶה יְיָ אֱלֹהֵינוּ וֵאלֹהֵי אֲבוֹתֵינוּ לְעוֹלָם וָעֶד: שִׁיר וּשְׁבָחָה, הַלֵּל וְזִמְרָה, עֹז וּמֶמְשָׁלָה, נֵצַח, גְּדֻלָּה וּגְבוּרָה, תְּהִלָּה וְתִפְאֶרֶת, קְדֻשָּׁה וּמַלְכוּת: בְּרָכוֹת וְהוֹדָאוֹת לְשִׁמְךָ הַגָּדוֹל וְהַקָּדוֹשׁ, וּמֵעוֹלָם עַד עוֹלָם אַתָּה אֵל. בָּרוּךְ אַתָּה יְיָ, אֵל מֶלֶךְ גָּדוֹל וּמְהֻלָּל בַּתִּשְׁבָּחוֹת, אֵל הַהוֹדָאוֹת, אֲדוֹן הַנִּפְלָאוֹת, בּוֹרֵא כָּל הַנְּשָׁמוֹת, רִבּוֹן כָּל הַמַּעֲשִׂים, הַבּוֹחֵר בְּשִׁירֵי זִמְרָה, מֶלֶךְ יָחִיד חֵי הָעוֹלָמִים:

הנוהגים לומר פזמונים אין להפסיק בהם בין ברכה זו ובין ברכת הכוס אלא מיד אחר כך יברך על כוס ד':

The cup is held in the palm of the right hand for the following blessing.

בָּרוּךְ אַתָּה יְיָ, אֱלֹהֵינוּ מֶלֶךְ הָעוֹלָם, בּוֹרֵא פְּרִי הַגָּפֶן:
ושותה בהסיבה:

Drink the entire cup without pause while seated, reclining on the left side. (One who cannot drink the entire cup should drink at least most of it.)

CONCLUDING BLESSING FOR WINE

On Friday night, add the words in shaded parentheses.

בָּרוּךְ אַתָּה יְיָ, אֱלֹהֵינוּ מֶלֶךְ הָעוֹלָם, עַל הַגֶּפֶן וְעַל פְּרִי הַגֶּפֶן וְעַל תְּנוּבַת הַשָּׂדֶה וְעַל אֶרֶץ חֶמְדָּה טוֹבָה וּרְחָבָה שֶׁרָצִיתָ וְהִנְחַלְתָּ לַאֲבוֹתֵינוּ לֶאֱכוֹל מִפִּרְיָהּ וְלִשְׂבּוֹעַ מִטּוּבָהּ. רַחֵם נָא יְיָ אֱלֹהֵינוּ עַל יִשְׂרָאֵל עַמֶּךְ וְעַל יְרוּשָׁלַיִם עִירֶךָ וְעַל צִיּוֹן מִשְׁכַּן

God and God of our fathers, to thank, to laud, to praise, to glorify, to exalt, to adore, to bless, to elevate and to honor You, even beyond all the words of songs and praises of David son of Yishai, Your anointed servant.

וּבְכֵן And therefore may Your Name be praised forever, our King, the great and holy God and King in heaven and on earth. For to You, GOD, our God and God of our fathers, forever befits song and praise, laud and hymn, strength and dominion, victory, greatness and might, glory, splendor, holiness and sovereignty; blessings and thanksgivings to Your great and holy Name; from the beginning to the end of the world You are Almighty God. Blessed are You, GOD, Almighty God, King, great and extolled in praises, God of thanksgivings, Lord of wonders, Creator of all souls, Master of all creatures, who takes pleasure in songs of praise; the only King, the Life of all worlds.

The cup is held in the palm of the right hand for the following blessing.

בָּרוּךְ Blessed are You, GOD, our God, King of the universe, who creates the fruit of the vine.

Drink the entire cup without pause while seated, reclining on the left side. (One who cannot drink the entire cup should drink at least most of it.)

CONCLUDING BLESSING FOR WINE

On Friday night, add the words in shaded parentheses.

בָּרוּךְ Blessed are You, GOD our God, King of the universe, for the vine and the fruit of the vine, for the produce of the field, and for the precious, good and spacious land which You have favored to give as a heritage to our fathers, to eat of its fruit and be satiated by its goodness. Have mercy, GOD our God, on Israel Your people, on Jerusalem Your city, on Zion the abode

כְּבוֹדֶךָ וְעַל מִזְבְּחֶךָ וְעַל הֵיכָלֶךָ, וּבְנֵה יְרוּשָׁלַיִם עִיר הַקֹּדֶשׁ בִּמְהֵרָה בְיָמֵינוּ, וְהַעֲלֵנוּ לְתוֹכָהּ וְשַׂמְּחֵנוּ בָהּ וּנְבָרֶכְךָ בִּקְדֻשָּׁה וּבְטָהֳרָה. (וּרְצֵה וְהַחֲלִיצֵנוּ בְּיוֹם הַשַּׁבָּת הַזֶּה.) וְזָכְרֵנוּ לְטוֹבָה בְּיוֹם חַג הַמַּצּוֹת הַזֶּה. כִּי אַתָּה יְיָ טוֹב וּמֵטִיב לַכֹּל וְנוֹדֶה לְּךָ עַל הָאָרֶץ וְעַל פְּרִי הַגָּפֶן. בָּרוּךְ אַתָּה יְיָ, עַל הָאָרֶץ וְעַל פְּרִי הַגָּפֶן:

CONCLUDING BLESSING FOR OTHER DRINKS, IF APPLICABLE

בָּרוּךְ אַתָּה יְיָ, אֱלֹהֵינוּ מֶלֶךְ הָעוֹלָם, בּוֹרֵא נְפָשׁוֹת רַבּוֹת וְחֶסְרוֹנָן, עַל כָּל מַה שֶּׁבָּרָאתָ לְהַחֲיוֹת בָּהֶם נֶפֶשׁ כָּל חַי, בָּרוּךְ חֵי הָעוֹלָמִים:

Afterwards say:

לְשָׁנָה הַבָּאָה בִּירוּשָׁלָיִם:

The wine in the "cup of Elijah" is poured back into the bottle.

of Your glory, on Your altar and on Your Temple. Rebuild Jerusalem, the holy city, speedily in our days, and bring us up into it, and make us rejoice in it, and we will bless You in holiness and purity. (May it please You to strengthen us on this Shabbat day.) And remember us for good on this day of the Festival of Matzot. For You, GOD, are good and do good to all, and we thank You for the land and for the fruit of the vine. Blessed are You, GOD, for the land and for the fruit of the vine.

CONCLUDING BLESSING FOR OTHER DRINKS, IF APPLICABLE

ברוך Blessed are You, GOD, our God, King of the universe, Who created numerous living beings and their needs, for all the things You have created with which to sustain the soul of every living being. Blessed is He who is the Life of all worlds.

Afterwards say:

NEXT YEAR IN JERUSALEM!

The wine in the "cup of Elijah" is poured back into the bottle.

Supplement

Mah Nishtanah:
Traditional Yiddish Rendition

טאַטע איך וועל בא דיר פרעגן פיר קשיות:

מַה נִשְׁתַּנָּה הַלַּיְלָה הַזֶּה מִכָּל הַלֵּילוֹת

וואָם איז אַנְדערש די נאכט פון פֶּסַח פון אַלֶע נֶעכט פון אַ
גאַנץ יאָר.

די עֶרשטע קשיא איז: שֶׁבְּכָל הַלֵּילוֹת אֵין אָנוּ מַטְבִּילִין אֲפִילוּ
פַּעַם אֶחָת הַלַּיְלָה הַזֶּה שְׁתֵּי פְעָמִים: אַלֶע נֶעכט פון אַ גאַנץ
יאָר טונקען מיר ניט אַיין אֲפִילוּ אֵיין מאָל, אָבֶּער די נאכט פון
פֶּסַח טונקען מיר אַיין צְווֵיי מאָל. אֵיין מאָל כַּרְפַּס אין זאַלץ
וואַסֶער דֶעם צְווֵייטן מאָל מָרוֹר אין חֲרֹסֶת.

די צְווֵייטע קשיא איז: שֶׁבְּכָל הַלֵּילוֹת אָנוּ אוֹכְלִין חָמֵץ אוֹ מַצָּה,
הַלַּיְלָה הַזֶּה כֻּלּוֹ מַצָּה: אַלֶע נֶעכט פון אַ גאַנץ יאָר עֶסן מיר
חָמֵץ אָדֶער מַצָּה, אָבֶּער די נאכט פון פֶּסַח עֶסן מיר נאָר מַצָּה.

די דריטע קשיא איז: שֶׁבְּכָל הַלֵּילוֹת אָנוּ אוֹכְלִין שְׁאָר יְרָקוֹת,
הַלַּיְלָה הַזֶּה מָרוֹר: אַלֶע נֶעכט פון אַ גאַנץ יאָר עֶסן מיר
אַנְדֶערע גְרִינסן, אָבֶּער די נאכט פון פֶּסַח עֶסן מיר בִּיטֶערע
גְרִינסן.

די פֶערטע קשיא איז: שֶׁבְּכָל הַלֵּילוֹת אָנוּ אוֹכְלִין בֵּין יוֹשְׁבִין
וּבֵין מְסֻבִּין, הַלַּיְלָה הַזֶּה כֻּלָּנוּ מְסֻבִּין: אַלֶע נֶעכט פון אַ גאַנץ
יאָר עֶסן מיר סַיי זִיצֶענְדיקֶערהֵייט און סַיי אָנְגֶעלֶענְטֶערהֵייט,
אָבֶּער די נאכט פון פֶּסַח עֶסן מיר נאָר אָנְגֶעלֶענְטֶערהֵייט.

טאַטע איך האָב בא דיר גֶעפְרֶעגְט פיר קשיות, יֶעצְט גיב מיר
אַן עֶנטפֶער.

Glossary

Afikoman: Lit., "Dessert." Piece of matzah taken from the Seder plate at the beginning of the Seder and kept hidden until the end of the meal; it is the last thing eaten before the Blessing After Meals—to commemorate the Pesach-offering (which was the last thing eaten at the Seder in the time of the *Beit Hamikdash*), or the matzah that had to be eaten with the Pesach-offering.

Alter Rebbe: Lit., "Elder Rebbe," R. Schneur Zalman of Liadi (1745-1812), author of *Tanya* and *Shulchan Aruch*, and founder of Chabad Chasidism.

Arizal: acronym for R. Yitzchak Luria (1534-1572); universally accepted father of modern Kabbalistic thought.

Beit Hamikdash: the Holy Temple of Jerusalem.

Beitzah: Lit., "Egg." Hardboiled egg placed on the Seder plate in commemoration of the *Chagigah* (festival-sacrifice) offered every festival in the time of the *Beit Hamikdash*.

Chakal Tapuchin: Kabbalistic term for a particular manifestation of the *Shechinah*.

Chametz: Leavened bread or substances. It is forbidden to enjoy, or even possess, any chametz from the eve of Pesach until the conclusion of Pesach.

Charoset: Mixture of grated apples, pears, nuts and red wine. The color and consistency of the charoset is to remind us of the clay and mortar with which our ancestors were forced to work in Egypt. The charoset is used as a dip for the maror and chazeret.

Chazeret: Commonly identified as romaine lettuce; used as one of the bitter herbs on the Seder plate to fulfill the obligations of Maror and Korech.

Eruv Tavshilin: Lit., "Mixture of cooked dishes." Procedure established by the Sages so that one may prepare food on a Festival for Shabbat.

Haggadah: Lit., "Narrative." Book containing the service at the Pesach Seder.

Hallel: Lit., "Psalms of Praise." Generally referring to Psalms 113-118. [More specifically we distinguish between *Hallel Mitzri* (the Hallel related to the exodus) Psalms 113-118, and *Hallel Hagadol*

(the Great Hallel)—Psalm 137 which praises God "enthroned in the heights of the universe and distributing food for all creatures." The unqualified term Hallel, however, always refers to *Hallel Mitzri*.]

Karpas: Umbelliferous vegetable like parsley, onion, potato, etc. (though excluding those that fall into the category of maror). It is eaten at the beginning of the Seder for the purpose of making the proceedings of the Seder night different, and thus stimulate the children's curiosity.

Ka'ara: Lit., "Tray" or "Platter." Used at the Seder for holding the matzot and the other requirements for the Seder.

Kelipah, pl. *Kelipot*: Lit., "Shell(s)." Kabbalistic term signifying evil and impurity. (For a detailed explanation see *Mystical Concepts in Chassidism*, ch. 10).

Kezayit, pl. *Kezeitim*: Lit., "Like an olive." Halachic term describing minimum size or amount for required consumption of certain edibles. At the Seder this measure is relevant to the eating of the matzah, maror, korech and the afikoman. It is also relevant to the eating of the karpas—of which one is to eat less than a *kezayit*. The dry measure of a *kezayit* is a fraction less than

an ounce (nearly 26 gram). See *Terms and Measurements* for more details.

Kiddush: Lit., "Sanctification." Blessing recited over a cup of wine, to sanctify the Shabbat or a Festival.

Kohen: Lit., "Priest." Member of the "priestly" class, i.e., descendants of Aaron the High Priest, in charge of the *Beit Hamikdash* and the sacrifices offered there. See below, under *Matzah*, and *Yisrael*.

Korech: Combination of matzah and maror, eaten like a sandwich before the meal, in memory of a procedure followed by Hillel the Elder in the time of the *Beit Hamikdash*.

Levi: Lit., "Levite." Descendants of the tribe of Levi (excluding the *Kohanim*), charged with assisting the *Kohanim* in the service and administration of the *Beit Hamikdash*. See below, under *Matzah*, and *Yisrael*.

Luria, R. Yitzchak: See above, under *Arizal*.

Maror: Bitter herbs, to be consumed at the Seder in commemoration of the bitter times suffered by our ancestors in Egypt. Both pure horseradish (cut into small pieces or grated) and chazeret are used for Maror.

Matzah, pl. *Matzot*: Unleavened

bread. Three matzot are to be placed on the Seder plate, symbolic of the three groups of Jews—*Kohanim, Levi'im,* and *Yisraelim*; or to recall our three patriarchs (Abraham, Isaac and Jacob); etc. On Pesach, at least for the Seder, one should use hand-baked matzot.

Nissan: Hebrew month in the spring.

Pesach: Passover.

Revi'it: Lit., "One fourth" [of a *log*]. Approximately 3.5 fluid ounces (nearly 105 milliliters).

Seder: Lit., "Order." The home service on the first two nights of Pesach.

Shechinah: Divine Presence or Indwelling.

Shochet: Ritual slaughterer.

Sitra Achara: Lit., "Other side." Kabbalistic term signifying evil and impurity. (For a detailed explanation see *Mystical Concepts in Chassidism*, ch. 10).

Yisrael: Israelite. Generally any Jew, but in the very specific sense one who is neither *Kohen* nor *Levi,* thus not a descendant of the tribe of Levi. In the context of the Seder this term appears in relation to the three matzot on the Seder plate—which are referred to as *Kohen, Levi* and *Yisrael*; see above, under matzah.

Z'eir Anpin: Kabbalistic term for a particular manifestation of the *Shechinah.*

Zeroa: Roasted bone of a lamb or fowl with some meat on it, placed on the Seder plate in commemoration of the Pesach-sacrifice offered in the time of the *Beit Hamikdash.* This bone is to be no more than a *symbolic reminder* of the Pesach-offering, and all similarities must be avoided. Thus it is our custom to use the neck of a chicken (which could not serve as a sacrifice), to remove most of its meat, and not to eat it during the Seder. For the same reason we do not eat roasted meat at all during the Seder.

Zimmun: Invitation recited before the Blessing After Meals, when at least three men are present.

Transliterations

Candle Lighting

Böruch atö adonöy, elohaynu melech hö-olöm, asher ki-d'shönu b'mitzvosöv, v'tzivönu l'hadlik nayr shel (shabös v'shel) yom tov.

Böruch atö adonöy, elohaynu melech hö-olöm, she-heche-yönu v'ki-y'mönu v'higi-önu li-z'man ha-ze.

Kiddush

On Friday night. Yom ha-shishi. Va-y'chulu ha-shöma-yim v'hö-öretz v'chöl tz'vö-öm. Va-y'chal elohim ba-yom ha-sh'vi-i, m'lachto asher ösö, va-yish-bos ba-yom ha-sh'vi-i miköl m'lachto asher, ösö. Va-y'vörech elo-him es yom ha-sh'vi-i, va-y'kadaysh oso, ki vo shövas miköl m'lachto, asher börö elohim la-asos.

Savri mörönön: Böruch atö adonöy elohaynu melech hö-olöm, boray p'ri ha-göfen.

Böruch atö adonöy elohaynu melech hö-olöm, asher böchar bönu mi-köl öm v'ro-m'mönu mi-köl löshon v'ki-d'shönu b'mitzvosöv, va-titen lönu adonöy elohaynu b'ahavö (shabösos lim'nuchö u-) mo-adim l'simchö chagim uz'manim l'söson, es yom (hashabos ha-ze, v'es yom) chag hamat-zos ha-ze, v'es yom tov mikrö kodesh ha-ze, z'man chayrusaynu (b'ahavö) mikrö kodesh zaycher li-tzi-as mitzrö-yim, ki vönu vöchartö v'osönu kidashtö miköl hö-amim, (v'shabös) u-mo-aday ködshechö (b'ahavö u-v'rötzon) b'simchö u-v'söson hinchaltönu. Böruch atö adonöy m'kadaysh (hashabös v') yisrö-ayl v'haz'manim.

On Saturday Night: Böruch atö adonöy elohaynu melech hö-olöm, boray m'oray hö-aysh.

Böruch atö adonöy elohaynu melech hö-olöm, hamavdil bayn kodesh l'chol, bayn or l'choshech, bayn yisrö-ayl lö-amim, bayn yom hash'vi-i l'shayshes y'may hama-ase. Bayn k'dushas shabös lik'dushas yom tov hiv-daltö, v'es yom hash'vi-i mi-shayshes y'may hama-ase kidashtö, hivdaltö v'kidashtö es am'chö yisrö-ayl bik'dushösechö. Böruch atö adonöy, hamavdil bayn kodesh l'kodesh.

Böruch atö adonöy, elohaynu melech hö-olöm, she-heche-yönu v'ki-y'mönu v'higi-önu li-z'man ha-ze.

Mah Nishtanah

Ma nishtana halai-lö ha-ze mikol halay-los?

Haggadah for Pesach

Sheb'chöl halay-los ayn önu matbilin afilu pa-am echös, halai-lö ha-ze sh'tay f'ömim.

Sheb'chöl halay-los önu och'lin chömaytz o matzö, halai-lö ha-ze kulo matzö.

Sheb'chöl halay-los önu och'lin sh'ör y'rökos, halai-lö ha-ze möror.

Sheb'chöl halay-los önu och'lin bayn yosh'vin uvayn m'subin, halai-lö ha-ze kulönu m'subin.

Vehi She'amdah

V'hi she-öm'dö la-avosaynu v'lönu, shelo echöd bil'vad ömad ölaynu l'chalosaynu, elö sheb'chöl dor vödor om'dim ölaynu l'chalosaynu, v'haködosh böruch hu matzilaynu mi-yödöm.

Dayenu

Ilu hotzi-önu mimitzra-yim v'lo ösö vöhem sh'fötim, da-yaynu.
Ilu ösö vöhem sh'fötim v'lo ösö vaylo-hayhem, da-yaynu.
Ilu ösö vaylo-hayhem v'lo hörag es b'chorayhem, da-yaynu.
Ilu hörag es b'chorayhem v'lo nösan lönu es mömonöm, da-yaynu.
Ilu nösan lönu es mömonöm v'lo köra lönu es ha-yöm, da-yaynu.
Ilu köra lönu es ha-yöm v'lo he-evirönu v'socho bechörövö, da-yaynu.
Ilu he-evirönu v'socho bechörövö v'lo shika tzöraynu b'socho, da-yaynu.
Ilu shika tzöraynu b'socho v'lo sipayk tzörkaynu bamidbör arbö-im shönö, da-yaynu.
Ilu sipayk tzörkaynu bamidbör arbö-im shönö v'lo he-echilönu es hamön, da-yaynu.
Ilu he-echilönu es hamön v'lo nösan lönu es ha-shabös, da-yaynu.
Ilu nösan lönu es ha-shabös v'lo kayr'vönu lif'nay har sinai, da-yaynu.
Ilu kayr'vönu lif'nay har sinai v'lo nösan lönu es hatorö, da-yaynu.
Ilu nösan lönu es hatorö v'lo hichnisönu l'eretz yisrö-ayl, da-yaynu.
Ilu hichnisönu l'eretz yisrö-ayl v'lo vönö lönu es bays hab'chirö, da-yaynu.

Rachtzah

Böruch atö adonöy elohaynu melech hö-olöm, asher kid'shönu b'mitzvosöv, v'tzivönu al n'tilas yödö-yim.

Motzi

Böruch atö adonöy elohaynu melech hö-olöm, hamotzi lechem min hö-öretz.

Matzah

Böruch atö adonöy elohaynu melech hö-olöm, asher kid'shönu b'mitzvosöv, v'tzivönu al achilas matzö.

109

Maror

Böruch atö adonöy elohaynu melech hö-olöm, asher kid'shönu b'mitzvosöv, v'tzivönu al achilas möror.

Korech

Kayn ösö hilayl biz'man shebays hamikdösh hö-yö ka-yöm, hö-yö koraych pesach matzö umöror v'ochayl b'yachad, k'mo shene-emar al matzos um'rorim yoch'lu-hu.

Zimmun

Leader: Rabosai mir vel'n bentsh'n.

Others: Y'hi shaym adonöy m'voröch may-atöh v'ad olöm.

Leader: Y'hi shaym adonöy m'voröch may-atöh v'ad olöm. Bir'shus mörönön v'rabönön v'rabosai, n'vöraych (elo-haynu) she-öchalnu mi-shelo.

Others who have eaten: Böruch (elo-haynu) she-öchalnu mi-shelo uv'tuvo chö-yinu.

Leader: Böruch (elo-haynu) she-öchalnu mi-shelo uv'tuvo chö-yinu.

Hodu

Hodu ladonöy ki tov, ki l'olöm chasdo.

Yomar nö yisrö-ayl, ki l'olöm chasdo.

Hodu ladonöy ki tov, ki l'olöm chasdo.

Yom'ru nö bays aharon, ki l'olöm chasdo.

Hodu ladonöy ki tov, ki l'olöm chasdo.

Yom'ru nö yir'ay adonöy, ki l'olöm chasdo.

Hodu ladonöy ki tov, ki l'olöm chasdo.

Ana Hashem

Önö adonöy hoshi-ö nö.
Önö adonöy hoshi-ö nö.

Önö adonöy hatzlichö nö.
Önö adonöy hatzlichö nö.

Keli Atah

Ayli atö v'odekö, elohai arom'mekö.
Hodu ladonöy ki tov, ki l'olöm chasdo.

L'shanah Haba'ah

L'shönö habö-ö birushölö-yim.

110

A Pesach Message
From the Lubavitcher Rebbe
Rabbi Menachem M. Schneerson
זצוקללה"ה נבג"מ זי"ע

The festival of Pesach calls for early and elaborate preparations to make the Jewish home fitting for the great festival. It is not physical preparedness alone that is required of us, but also spiritual preparedness—for in the life of the Jew the physical and spiritual are closely linked together, especially in the celebration of our Sabbath and festivals.

On Pesach we celebrate the liberation of the Jewish people from Egyptian slavery and, together with it, the liberation from, and negation of the ancient Egyptian system and way of life, the "abominations of Egypt." Thus we celebrate our physical liberation together with our spiritual freedom. Indeed, there cannot be one without the other; there can be no real freedom without accepting the precepts of our Torah guiding our daily life; pure and holy life eventually leads to real freedom.

It is said: "In every generation each Jew should see himself as though he personally had been liberated from Egypt." This is to say, that the lesson of Pesach has always a timely message for the individual Jew. The story of Pesach is the story of the special Divine Providence which alone determines the fate of our people. What is happening in the outside world need not affect us; we might be singled out for suffering, G-d forbid, amid general prosperity, and likewise singled out for safety amid a general plague or catastrophe. The story of our enslavement and liberation of which Pesach tells

us, gives ample illustration of this. For th. is determined by its adherence to G-d and His Prophets.

This lesson is emphasized by the three principal symbols of the Seder, concerning which our Sages said that unless the Jew explains their significance he has not observed the Seder fittingly: Pesach, Matzah and Maror. Using these symbols in their chronological order and in accordance with the Haggadah explanation we may say: the Jews avoid Maror (bitterness of life) only through Pesach (G-d's special care 'passing over' and saving the Jewish homes even in the midst of the greatest plague), and Matzah—then the very catastrophe and the enemies of the Jews will work for the benefit of the Jews, driving them in great haste out of "Mitzrayim," the place of perversion and darkness, and placing them under the beam of light and holiness.

One other important thing we must remember. The celebration of the festival of freedom must be connected with the commandment, "You shall relate it to Your son." The formation and existence of the Jewish home, as of the Jewish people as a whole, is dependent upon the upbringing of the young generation, both boys and girls: the wise and the wicked (temporarily), the simple and the one who knows not what to ask. Just as we cannot shirk our responsibility towards our child by the excuse that "my child is a wise one; he will find his own way in life therefore no education is necessary for him;" so we must not despair by thinking "the child is a wicked one; no education will help him." For, all Jewish children, boys and girls, are "G-d's children" and it is our sacred duty to see to it that they all live up to their above mentioned title; and this we can achieve only through a kosher Jewish education, in full adherence to G-d's Torah. Then we all will merit the realization of our ardent hopes: "In the next year may we be free; in the next year may we be in Jerusalem!"

RABBI MENACHEM M. SCHNEERSON